moroccan
food & cooking

moroccan
food & cooking

traditions · tastes · techniques · 75 classic recipes

Ghillie Başan

contents

the ancient roots of a modern cuisine   6

mezze & soups   10

street food   34

couscous & tagines   58

roasts, grills & pan-fried dishes   82

salads & side dishes   108

sweets, pastries & drinks   126

basic flavourings & ingredients   150

index   158

credits & acknowledgements   160

the ancient roots of a modern cuisine

There are some cuisines in the world that, undoubtedly, make me feel hungry when I think about them. The cuisine of Morocco is certainly one of them. With its sweet and spicy combinations, and its exciting use of cumin and coriander, honey and ginger, saffron and cinnamon, chillies and turmeric, and olives and preserved lemons, it is both inspirational and divine. It is the perfumed soul of our culture, says the Moroccan-born writer Edmond Amran el Maleh. Moroccan food and cooking is also a fascinating reflection of the history of a country whose invaders have come and gone, each leaving a stamp on the cuisine.

Morocco is a vast country of desert, rugged mountainous terrain, fertile inland and coastal plains, with the Atlantic Ocean and Mediterranean Sea lapping its shores. The influences of the past can clearly be seen in modern Morocco cuisine – from the traditional foods that have been eaten for millenia to the contribution made by different cultures and evolving trade.

The first inhabitants of the Maghreb – the Arab term for the countries of North Africa – are thought to have dwelled in the Sahara as hunter-gatherers. Recorded history begins around 1100BC with the ancient Phoenicians, who set up trading colonies along the coastlines, from where they traded saffron, which was used as a dye in ancient Egypt. However, as most of their colonies were built on defensible headlands, they probably had little contact with the indigenous population of Berbers who inhabited the inland fertile plains and harsh mountainous terrain, where they lived off honey, beans, lentils and wheat. The Carthaginians were the next to take over the African trading routes and developed some of the ports into considerable cities, exporting grain and grapes, as well as minting their own coinage. After Carthage was sacked in the Punic Wars, the Romans incorporated the region into their

empire as the province of Mauritiana. Later, when the Roman legions withdrew, the Vandals took power in southern Spain and controlled some of the North African ports before they were defeated by the Byzantines.

None of these empires were to have such an impact on the region and its culinary history as the new force rising in the East – the Arabs and Islam. Not long after the death of the Prophet Mohammed in 632AD, the Arabs arrived in the Maghreb and brought about significant changes as they converted the inhabitants to Islam and their own culinary culture. They brought spices from the East, rice from India, the Persian habit of combining meat and fruit in stews, the idea of the scented broth, and the tradition of mezze – a spread of appetizers.

In Algeria, the Berbers, including integrated Jews and Coptic Christians from Egypt, put up a resistance for a while but, by the early part of 700AD, most of the inhabitants had embraced Islam, and North Africa was effectively under Arab rule. With their Berber recruits, the Arabs began to look for new territories to conquer and convert, and, like the Romans and Byzantines before them, their main thrust was towards Spain. So began the significant and lasting cultural and culinary influence of the Moors (the term for people of mixed Berber and Arab descent)

on southern Spain, Portugal and Sicily. Around the time that Columbus was landing in the Americas, the Moors were forced from al-Andaluz (Andalucia) to return to Morocco, where they spread their acquired Spanish culinary and cultural influences. Beginning in Tangier and Tetouan, they spread to the courts of Fez and south to Marrakesh. By the time the Ottoman Empire spread across North Africa, the cuisine of Morocco was established, so the sophisticated cooking from the palace kitchens of Istanbul did not alter it, but added to it.

Today, Morocco is a culinary haven. In the north of the country, in cities such as Tangier and Tetouan, there is a Spanish influence in the language, architecture and food. In Fez, the most complete medieval city of the Arab world, the senses are stimulated by the haunting sounds and hypnotizing odours. This city has dominated Moroccan trade, culture and religious life since the end of the tenth century and its cuisine is a unique reflection of the diversity of its inhabitants, which have included Berbers, Jews, Arabs, Andalusians, the French and other Europeans. Casablanca, the principal city of Morocco and the largest port in the Maghreb, is cosmopolitan in its style and food. Further south, in Marrakesh, Safi, and Essaouira, the culinary influences come from Africa and the Atlantic. Marrakesh was once a trading post for slaves from Sudan, Senegal and the ancient kingdom of Timbuktu, as well as a

market place for the goods of Atlas tribes, Maghrebis from the plains, and nomads from the Sahara. It is particularly interesting for its Berber, rather than Arab, origins, which are reflected in the low, red buildings as well as the food. Inland though, in the harsher terrain of the Rif, the Atlas and the southern oases, there has been little outside influence and the nomadic Berber tribes still hold on to their ancient cultural and culinary identity.

In every Moroccan home, palatial or modest, old or modern, the family meal is served at a low table surrounded by benches or cushions. The dishes are placed in the centre of the table, often in the earthenware dishes in which they were cooked, and everyone tucks in. Traditionally, there is no crockery or cutlery, although this has changed in many modern households. Instead, the right thumb, index and middle fingers are used to scoop up the food, along with plenty of bread to mop up the juices.

Most meals begin with a simple selection of mezze, which might include a bowl of olives, a cooked vegetable salad dressed with olive oil, sprinkled with cumin, and served with a dip, flat bread and a savoury pastry. The tagines or a roast meat dish may come next, often served with a punchy, fresh raw salad to soothe the palate. Couscous may follow but

traditionally, when couscous is accompanied by a stew or broth, it is usually reserved for a meal on its own. A simple plate of prepared fresh fruit or dessert marks the end of the meal before mint tea is served.

The room where the food is cooked displays none of the grandeur or exoticism of the actual dishes, as a traditional Moroccan kitchen is semi-dark, cool in the heat of summer and damp in winter. The cooking utensils are simple, either glazed earthenware tagines or copper pots. There is an old stove fired by charcoal, which blackens the tiled walls but cooks gently, and a portable *kanoun*, a brazier made of sun-baked clay.

In a household that can afford servants, the cooks are often women, descended from slaves brought from Sudan, as their culinary skills are held in high esteem. The dripping water in the fountain and the bashing of the pestle and mortar fill the darkness of the kitchen, along with the pungent, aromatic odour of garlic and spices perfumed with a whiff of rose or mint. This kitchen is like a magician's cave, where Allah's blessing is sought before every delightful dish is conjured up. Of course, the modern kitchens of the more Europeanized households lack this ambience but most Moroccan women still take great pride in their cooking.

When visiting the country, one of the most exciting ways of sampling a variety of mouthwatering dishes is to attend a feast, called a *diffa*. This may involve half a dozen dishes rising to as many as twenty courses for a special feast to celebrate, for example, a wedding or circumcision. Traditionally, the guests sit on cushions around a low table. The first dish to be served is the impressive *bistilla*, a round, layered, paper-thin pastry enclosing two savoury fillings of stewed pigeon and spices, and one sweet filling of sautéed almonds with icing (confectioners') sugar and cinnamon. The *bistilla* is fried in butter on both sides, sprinkled with sugar and cinnamon in a decorative pattern, and served on a platter in the middle of the table.

The second dish of a *diffa* is usually a *choua*, a steamed shoulder of lamb flavoured with cumin or, in the countryside, a *mechoui*, a whole roast lamb or goat cooked over glowing coals in a pit in the ground. Next come a variety of tagines, each one different, served with flat bread to mop up the tasty sauce. The last tagine is always sweet, usually made of lamb, caramelized onions and honey. Just to make sure that no guest leaves with any space unfilled, the grand finale is a steaming mound of couscous, also eaten with the fingers. Mint tea, the classic Moroccan drink, is served afterwards to refresh the palate and aid digestion.

One of the most interesting ways to absorb the delights and diversity of a country's cuisine is to visit the markets. They are cool, spicy, colourful and noisy. Gleaming, ripe vegetables and fruit are piled high; long, leafy herbs are tied in bundles; simple white and yellow cheeses and slabs of butter are stacked in blocks; olive oil and local olives steep in deep vats; pickles, conserves and preserved lemons are displayed in huge jars or bowls; and there are nuts and dried fruit laid out, begging to be sampled and nibbled. The most remarkable of all the markets are the old, labyrinthine souks of Fez and Marrakesh where, among the dangling snake skins and other natural remedies of the apothecary, the drying lavender and rose buds, the most enticing characteristic is the aroma of exotic spices.

With such a rich and diverse culinary history, which draws from the East, the Mediterranean and tropical Africa, Morocco is home to some of the most tantalizing food imaginable. The dishes are designed to please the eye as well as the palate, intoxicating you with their heady spices and sumptuous sauces. Simple, traditional cooking methods and classic spice mixes mean that it is easy to produce the flavours of Morocco at home. Whether you want to make a quick meal or prepare a lavish feast, the wonderful collection of recipes in this book will allow you to recreate the scents and flavours of Morocco.

mezze
& soups

whetting the appetite

The ancient tradition of mezze was probably introduced to Morocco by the Arabs in the seventh century. Derived from the Persian word *maza*, meaning taste or relish, this course was intended to delight the palate before the main meal. Eating mezze remains one of the most wonderful ways of eating Middle Eastern and North African food today.

The combination of simple dishes, complex flavours and the relaxed style of mezze eating is now enjoyed all over the world. There is no rush as you sample a selection of dishes that might include a bowl of freshly roasted pistachios, succulent and flavourful marinated olives, roasted (bell) peppers bathed in olive oil, garlicky dip made with yogurt and flavoured with fiery harissa, small, delicate pastries filled with cinnamon-flavoured minced (ground) lamb, and a fresh salad flavoured with preserved lemon.

Like mezze, soups are often served before the main meal to whet the appetite. Everyday fare in a household may consist of one main dish, possibly a tagine or couscous, to follow a light soup. However, soups may also be hearty enough to make a meal in themselves, served with lots of bread.

The classic flavours of Moroccan cooking – ginger, coriander, cumin, cinnamon, garlic, paprika, orange flower water, preserved lemons and ras el hanout – all feature in the mezze and soups, stimulating the appetite for the ensuing courses.

Moroccans are renowned for their hospitality and they go to great lengths to make sure guests are comfortable and offered food and refreshment. This may involve a few appetizing dishes to display the season's best ingredients or mark the beginning of a long night of eating many courses.

When preparing a Moroccan meal, start with a selection of appetizers that are quite different from each other, such as grilled aubergine slices cooked in honey and spices, a garlicky dip, and a fresh, raw salad. The contrasting yet complementary tastes and textures reflect the true flavour of Morocco food.

zahlouk and pale courgette and cauliflower salad

Zahlouk is a delicious, spicy aubergine and tomato salad that can be made with olive oil or argan oil, which is pressed from the nut found inside the fruit of the argan tree indigenous to the Souss region of Morocco. I often serve zahlouk as an appetizer, with lots of bread to scoop it up, but it also sits beautifully in a mezze spread. Cauliflower and courgettes are a popular combination in Morocco; served in salads, grilled on skewers, and added to couscous and tagines.

FOR THE ZAHLOUK
3 large aubergines (eggplant),
    peeled and cubed
3–4 large tomatoes, peeled and
    chopped to a pulp
5ml/1 tsp sugar
3–4 garlic cloves, crushed
60ml/4 tbsp olive oil or argan oil
juice of 1 lemon
scant 5ml/1 tsp harissa
5ml/1 tsp cumin seeds, roasted
    and ground
small bunch of flat leaf
    parsley, chopped
salt

FOR THE COURGETTE AND
CAULIFLOWER SALAD
1 cauliflower, broken into florets
2–3 small courgettes (zucchini),
    thickly sliced
60ml/4 tbsp olive oil
juice of 1 lemon
2–3 garlic cloves, crushed
small bunch of parsley,
    finely chopped
salt and ground black pepper
5ml/1 tsp paprika, to serve

SERVES 4

To make the zahlouk, boil the aubergines in plenty of salted water for about 15 minutes, until they are very soft. Drain and squeeze out the excess water, then chop and mash them with a fork.

Put the pulped tomatoes in a pan, stir in the sugar, and cook over a gentle heat until they are reduced to a thick sauce. Add the mashed aubergines. Stir in the garlic, olive or argan oil, lemon juice, harissa, cumin and parsley until thoroughly mixed. Season to taste.

To make the courgette and cauliflower salad, heat about half the olive oil in a heavy pan and brown the courgettes on both sides. Drain on kitchen paper.

Meanwhile, steam the cauliflower over boiling water for 7–10 minutes until tender. While the cauliflower is still warm, mash it lightly in a bowl and mix in the remaining olive oil, half the lemon juice and the garlic. Add the courgettes and parsley with the remaining lemon juice and season to taste.

Serve the zahlouk at room temperature with plenty of flat bread. Serve the courgette and cauliflower salad warm or at room temperature, sprinkled with paprika.

bissara dip with zahtar

This garlicky broad bean dip is enjoyed throughout Morocco. Sprinkled with the Middle-Eastern spice zahtar, paprika or dried thyme, it makes a tasty appetizer served with flat bread. It is particularly popular in the cafés of Fez and Marrakesh, where Moroccans and tourists mingle over food.

Drain the beans, remove their wrinkly skins and place them in a large pan with the garlic and cumin seeds. Add enough water to cover the beans and bring to the boil. Boil for 10 minutes, then reduce the heat, cover the pan and simmer gently for about 1 hour, or until the beans are tender.

When cooked, drain the beans and, while they are still warm, pound or process them with the olive oil until the mixture forms a smooth dip. Season to taste with salt and serve warm or at room temperature, sprinkled with zahtar, paprika or thyme. Alternatively, simply drizzle with a little olive oil.

350g/12oz/1¾ cups dried broad
  (fava) beans, soaked overnight
4 garlic cloves
10ml/2 tsp cumin seeds
60–75ml/4–5 tbsp olive oil
salt
zahtar, paprika or dried thyme
  to garnish

SERVES 4

roasted red peppers with feta, capers and preserved lemons

Roasted red peppers, particularly the long, slim, horn-shaped type, feature widely across the Middle East and Mediterranean regions. However, it is the delightful burst of piquant fruit that gives these sumptuous roast peppers their typically Moroccan flavour. So versatile and juicy, they are quite delicious with kebabs and barbecued meats as well as with other mezze dishes.

4 fleshy, red (bell) peppers
200g/7oz feta cheese, crumbled
30–45ml/2–3 tbsp olive oil or
    argan oil
30ml/2 tbsp capers
peel of 1 preserved lemon, cut into
    small pieces
salt

SERVES 4

Preheat the grill (broiler) on the hottest setting. Roast the red peppers under the grill, turning frequently, until they soften and their skins begin to blacken. (Alternatively, spear the peppers, one at a time, on long metal skewers and turn them over a gas flame, or roast them in a very hot oven.) Place the peppers in a plastic bag, seal and leave them to stand for 15 minutes. Peel the peppers, remove the stalks and seeds, then slice the flesh and arrange on a plate.

Add the crumbled feta and pour over the olive or argan oil. Scatter the capers and preserved lemon over the top and sprinkle with a little salt, if required (this depends on whether the feta is salty or not). Serve with chunks of fresh bread to mop up the delicious, oil-rich juices.

artichoke hearts with ginger, honey and preserved lemons

When globe artichokes are in season, they grace every Moroccan table as a first course or salad. The hearts are often poached in salted water until tender, chopped and tossed in olive oil with garlic, herbs and preserved lemon. For a more exciting appetizer, the artichokes are cooked in a glorious spiced honey dressing. This dish also makes a perfect accompaniment for barbecued meat.

Heat the olive oil in a small heavy pan and stir in the garlic. Before the garlic begins to colour, stir in the ginger, saffron, lemon juice, honey and preserved lemon. Add the artichokes and toss them in the spices and honey. Pour in the water, add a little salt and heat until simmering.

Cover the pan and simmer for 10–15 minutes until the artichokes are tender, turning them occasionally. If the liquid has not reduced, take the lid off the pan and boil for about 2 minutes until reduced to a coating consistency. Serve warm or at room temperature.

Preparing globe artichokes
Remove the outer leaves and cut off the stems. Carefully separate the remaining leaves and use a teaspoon to scoop out the choke with all the hairy bits. Trim the hearts and immerse them in water mixed with a squeeze of lemon juice to prevent them from turning black. Frozen prepared hearts are available in some supermarkets and they can be used for this recipe.

30–45ml/2–3 tbsp olive oil
2 garlic cloves, crushed
scant 5ml/1 tsp ground ginger
pinch of saffron threads
juice of ½ lemon
15–30ml/1–2 tbsp honey
peel of 1 preserved lemon,
    finely sliced
8 artichoke hearts, quartered
150ml/¼ pint/⅔ cup water
salt

SERVES 4

grilled aubergine in honey and spices

Hot, spicy, sweet and fruity are classic flavours of North African cooking and in this delicious Moroccan dish, their combination sends you on a thrilling journey. For a spread of tantalizing tastes, serve with artichoke heart and orange salad and the garlicky dip, bissara. Baby aubergines are very effective for this dish as you can slice them in half lengthways and hold them by their stalks.

Preheat the grill (broiler) or a griddle. Dip each aubergine slice in olive oil and cook in a pan under the grill or in a griddle pan. Turn the slices so that they are lightly browned on both sides.

In a wide frying pan, fry the garlic in a little olive oil for a few seconds, then stir in the ginger, cumin, harissa, honey and lemon juice. Add enough water to cover the base of the pan and to thin the mixture, then lay the aubergine slices in the pan. Cook the aubergines gently for about 10 minutes, or until they have absorbed all the sauce.

Add a little extra water, if necessary, season to taste with salt, and serve at room temperature, with chunks of fresh bread to mop up the juices.

Alternative flavourings
Courgettes (zucchini) can also be cooked in this way. If you want to make a feature out of this sumptuous dish, serve it with other grilled (broiled) vegetables and fruit, such as (bell) peppers, chillies, tomatoes, oranges, pineapple and mangoes.

2 aubergines (eggplant), peeled and thickly sliced
olive oil, for frying
2–3 garlic cloves, crushed
5cm/2in piece of fresh root ginger, peeled and grated
5ml/1 tsp ground cumin
5ml/1 tsp harissa
75ml/5 tbsp clear honey
juice of 1 lemon
salt

SERVES 4

pan-fried baby squid with spices

8 baby squid, prepared,
  with tentacles
5ml/1 tsp ground turmeric
15ml/1 tbsp smen or olive oil
2 garlic cloves, finely chopped
15g/½oz fresh root ginger, peeled
  and finely chopped
5–10ml/1–2 tsp honey
juice of 1 lemon
10ml/2 tsp harissa
salt
small bunch of fresh coriander
  (cilantro), roughly chopped,
  to serve

SERVES 4

You have to work quickly to prepare this dish, then serve it immediately, so that the squid is just cooked and tender. The flavours of turmeric, ginger and harissa are fabulous with the sweet honey and zesty lemon juice.

Pat dry the squid bodies, inside and out, and dry the tentacles. Sprinkle the squid and tentacles with the ground turmeric.

Heat the smen or olive oil in a large heavy frying pan and stir in the garlic and ginger. Just as the ginger and garlic begin to colour, add the squid and tentacles and fry quickly on both sides over a high heat. (Don't overcook the squid, otherwise it will become rubbery.)

Add the honey, lemon juice and harissa and stir to form a thick, spicy, caramelized sauce. Season with salt, sprinkle with the chopped coriander and serve immediately.

hot spicy prawns with coriander

This is a quick and easy way of preparing prawns for a snack or appetizer. If you increase the quantities, it can be served as a main course. Scallops and mussels are also delicious cooked in this way or, alternatively, you can select a variety of mushrooms and add them to the pan with the sauce ingredients. Serve the prawns with bread to mop up the tasty juices.

In a large, heavy frying pan, heat the oil with the garlic. Stir in the ginger, chilli and cumin seeds. Cook briefly, until the ingredients give off a lovely aroma, then add the paprika and toss in the prawns.

Fry the prawns over a fairly high heat, turning them frequently, for 3–5 minutes, until just cooked. Season to taste with salt and add the coriander. Serve immediately, with lemon wedges for squeezing over the prawns.

60ml/4 tbsp olive oil
2–3 garlic cloves, chopped
25g/1oz fresh root ginger, peeled
   and shredded
1 chilli, seeded and chopped
5ml/1 tsp cumin seeds
5ml/1 tsp paprika
450g/1lb uncooked king prawns
   (jumbo shrimp), shelled
bunch of fresh coriander
   (cilantro), chopped
salt
1 lemon, cut into wedges, to serve

SERVES 2–4

mini saffron fish cakes with chilled sweet cucumber and cinnamon salad

This scented cucumber salad makes a superbly refreshing accompaniment for the fish cakes. Both the fish cakes and salad include the sweet and spicy flavours that are so popular in Moroccan food. If you're in a rush and can't get fresh fish, canned tuna makes a good substitute.

Make the salad in advance to allow time for chilling before serving. Place the cucumber in a strainer over a bowl and sprinkle with some salt. Leave to drain for about 10 minutes. Using your hands, squeeze out the excess liquid and place the cucumber in a bowl.

In a small jug (pitcher), combine the orange and lemon juice, orange flower water and sugar and pour over the cucumber. Toss well, sprinkle with cinnamon and chill for at least 1 hour.

To make the fish cakes, put the fish in a food processor. Add the harissa, preserved lemon, coriander, egg, honey, saffron with its soaking water, and seasoning, and whizz until smooth. Divide the mixture into 16 portions. Wet your hands under cold water to prevent the mixture from sticking to them, then roll each portion into a ball and flatten in the palm of your hand.

Heat the oil in a large frying pan and fry the fish cakes in batches, until golden brown on each side. Drain the fish cakes on kitchen paper and keep hot until all the fish cakes are cooked. Serve immediately with the chilled cucumber salad.

450g/1lb white fish fillets, such as
   sea bass, ling or haddock,
   skinned and cut into chunks
10ml/2 tsp harissa
rind of ½ preserved lemon,
   finely chopped
small bunch fresh coriander
   (cilantro), finely chopped
1 egg
5ml/1 tsp honey
pinch of saffron threads, soaked
   in 5ml/1 tsp water
salt and ground black pepper
sunflower oil, for frying

FOR THE SALAD
2 cucumbers, peeled and grated
juice of 1 orange
juice of ½ lemon
15–30ml/1–2 tbsp orange
   flower water
15–20ml/3–4 tsp sugar
2.5ml/½ tsp ground cinnamon

SERVES 4

sautéed chicken livers with orange flower water and roasted hazelnuts

Sautéed offal, such as liver and kidney, is a popular appetizer, often cooked simply in olive oil and garlic and served with lemon to squeeze over. This dish of chicken livers makes a delicious, tangy appetizer on its own, served with a few salad leaves, or spooned on thin slices of toasted bread. In the restaurants of Casablanca, where the French influence still lingers, the refinement of this dish is much enjoyed.

Heat the olive oil in a heavy frying pan and stir in the garlic, chilli and cumin seeds. Add the chicken livers and toss over the heat until they are browned on all sides. Reduce the heat a little and continue to cook for 3–5 minutes.

When the livers are almost cooked, add the ground coriander and hazelnuts. Stir in the orange flower water and preserved lemon. Season to taste with salt and black pepper and serve immediately, sprinkled with a little fresh coriander.

Variation
Lamb's liver, trimmed and finely sliced, is also good cooked this way. The trick is to sear the outside so that the middle is almost pink and melts in the mouth. If you don't have orange flower water, try a little balsamic vinegar.

30–45ml/2–3 tbsp olive oil
2–3 garlic cloves, chopped
1 dried red chilli, chopped
5ml/1 tsp cumin seeds
450g/1lb chicken livers, trimmed
    and cut into bitesize chunks
5ml/1 tsp ground coriander
handful of roasted hazelnuts,
    roughly chopped
10–15ml/2–3 tsp orange
    flower water
½ preserved lemon, finely sliced
    or chopped
salt and ground black pepper
small bunch of fresh coriander
    (cilantro), finely chopped,
    to serve

SERVES 4

cinnamon-scented chickpea and lentil soup with fennel and honey buns

This thick pulse and vegetable soup, flavoured with ginger and cinnamon, varies from village to village and town to town. It is believed to have originated from a semolina gruel that the Berbers prepared to warm themselves during the cold winters in the Atlas Mountains. Over the centuries, it has been adapted and refined with spices and tomatoes from the New World.

30–45ml/2–3 tbsp smen or olive oil
2 onions, halved and sliced
2.5ml/½ tsp ground ginger
2.5ml/½ tsp ground turmeric
5ml/1 tsp ground cinnamon
pinch of saffron threads
2 × 400g/14oz cans chopped
    tomatoes
5–10ml/1–2 tsp caster
    (superfine) sugar
175g/6oz/¾ cup brown or green
    lentils, picked over and rinsed
about 1.75 litres/3 pints/7½ cups
    meat or vegetable stock, or water
200g/7oz/1 generous cup dried
    chickpeas, soaked overnight,
    drained and boiled until tender
200g/7oz/1 generous cup dried
    broad (fava) beans, soaked
    overnight, drained and boiled
    until tender
small bunch of fresh coriander
    (cilantro), chopped
small bunch of flat leaf
    parsley, chopped
salt and ground black pepper

FOR THE BUNS
2.5ml/½ tsp dried yeast
300g/11oz/1¼ cups unbleached
    strong white bread flour
15–30ml/1–2 tbsp clear honey
5ml/1 tsp fennel seeds
250ml/8fl oz/1 cup milk
1 egg yolk, stirred with a little milk
salt

SERVES 8

Make the fennel and honey buns. Dissolve the yeast in about 15ml/1 tbsp lukewarm water. Sift the flour and a pinch of salt into a bowl. Make a well in the centre and add the dissolved yeast, honey and fennel seeds. Gradually pour in the milk, using your hands to work it into the flour along with the honey and yeast, until the mixture forms a dough – if the dough becomes too sticky to handle add more flour.

Turn the dough out on to a floured surface and knead well for about 10 minutes, until it is smooth and elastic. Flour the surface under the dough and cover it with a damp cloth, then leave the dough to rise until it has doubled in size.

Preheat the oven to 230°C/450°F/Gas 8. Grease two baking sheets. Divide the dough into 12 balls. On a floured surface, flatten the balls of dough with the palm of your hand, then place them on a baking sheet. Brush the tops of the buns with egg yolk, then bake for about 15 minutes until they are risen slightly and sound hollow when tapped underneath. Transfer to a wire rack to cool.

To make the soup, heat the smen or olive oil in a stockpot or large pan. Add the onions and stir for about 15 minutes, or until they are soft.

Add the ginger, turmeric, cinnamon and saffron, followed by the tomatoes and a little sugar. Stir in the lentils and pour in the stock or water. Bring the liquid to the boil, then reduce the heat, cover and simmer for about 25 minutes, or until the lentils are tender.

Stir in the cooked chickpeas and beans, bring back to the boil, then cover and simmer for a further 10–15 minutes. Stir in the fresh herbs and season the soup to taste. Serve piping hot, with the fennel and honey buns.

Allowing preparation time
A little advance preparation is required for this soup: the dried chickpeas and beans have to be soaked for about 8 hours and then cooked in lots of water until tender. To achieve the authentic flavour of this peasant dish, it is also well worth making smen, the classic Moroccan aged butter. The fennel and honey buns can be made big or small and, if you make enough of them, they are also delicious served with honey or cheese for breakfast or lunch.

chilled almond and garlic soup
with roasted chilli and grapes

The cold and chilled soups of North Africa are ancient in origin and were originally introduced to Morocco by the Arabs. This particular milky white soup has travelled further with the Moors into Spain. Heavily laced with garlic, it is unusual but deliciously refreshing in hot weather, and makes a delightful, tangy first course for a summer lunch party.

Place the blanched almonds in a food processor and blend to form a smooth paste. Add the bread, garlic, olive oil and half the water and process again until smooth. With the motor running, continue adding the rest of the water in a slow, steady stream until the mixture is smooth with the consistency of single (light) cream. Add vinegar and salt to taste. Chill for at least 1 hour, then serve garnished with the sliced roasted chilli, grapes and almonds.

130g/4½ oz/ generous 1 cup
  blanched almonds
3–4 slices day-old white bread,
  crusts removed
4 garlic cloves
60ml/4 tbsp olive oil
about 1 litre/1½ pints/4 cups
  iced water
30ml/2 tbsp white wine vinegar
salt

TO GARNISH
1 dried red chilli, roasted and
  finely sliced
a small bunch of sweet green grapes,
  halved and seeded
a handful blanched almonds

SERVES 4

velvety pumpkin soup
with rice and cinnamon

Modern Moroccan streets and markets are full of colourful seasonal produce that inspire you to buy, go home and start cooking. The pumpkin season is particularly delightful, with the huge orange vegetables piled up on stalls and wooden carts. The sellers patiently peel and slice the pumpkins ready for making this delicious winter soup.

Remove any seeds or fibre from the pumpkin, cut off the peel and chop the flesh. Put the prepared pumpkin in a pan and add the stock, milk, sugar and seasoning. Bring to the boil, then reduce the heat and simmer for about 20 minutes, or until the pumpkin is tender. Drain the pumpkin, reserving the liquid, and purée it in a food processor, then return it to the pan.

Bring the soup back to the boil again, throw in the rice and simmer for a few minutes, until the grains are reheated. Check the seasoning, dust with cinnamon and pour into bowls. Serve piping hot, with chunks of bread.

about 1.1kg/2lb 7oz pumpkin
750ml/1¼ pints/3 cups
    chicken stock
750ml/1¼ pints/3 cups milk
10–15ml/2–3 tsp sugar
75g/3oz/½ cup cooked white rice
salt and ground black pepper
5ml/1 tsp ground cinnamon,
    to serve

SERVES 4

chunky tomato soup
with ras el hanout and noodles

This full-flavoured *chorba* is the daily soup in many Moroccan households. The ras el hanout gives it a lovely, warming kick. You can purée the soup, if you prefer, but I like it just as it is, finished off with a swirl of yogurt and finely chopped coriander. Garlic lovers may like to add a crushed garlic clove and a little salt to the yogurt. Serve with chunks of fresh bread.

In a deep, heavy pan, heat the oil and add the cloves, onions, squash, celery and carrots. Fry until they begin to colour, then stir in the tomatoes and sugar. Cook the tomatoes until the water reduces and they begin to pulp.

Stir in the tomato purée, ras el hanout, turmeric and chopped coriander. Pour in the stock and bring the liquid to the boil. Reduce the heat and simmer for 30–40 minutes until the vegetables are very tender and the liquid has reduced a little.

To make a puréed soup, leave the liquid to cool slightly before processing in a food processor or blender, then pour back into the pan and add the pasta. Alternatively, to make a chunky soup, simply add the pasta to the unblended soup and cook for a further 8–10 minutes, or until the pasta is soft. Season the soup to taste and ladle it into bowls. Spoon a swirl of yogurt into each one, garnish with the extra coriander and serve with a freshly baked Moroccan loaf.

45–60ml/3–4 tbsp olive oil
3–4 cloves
2 onions, chopped
1 butternut squash, peeled, seeded
    and cut into small chunks
4 celery stalks, chopped
2 carrots, peeled and chopped
8 large, ripe tomatoes, skinned
    and roughly chopped
5–10ml/1–2 tsp sugar
15ml/1 tbsp tomato purée (paste)
5–10ml/1–2 tsp ras el hanout
2.5ml/½ tsp ground turmeric
1.8 litres/3 pints/7 ½ cups
    vegetable stock
a big bunch of fresh coriander
    (cilantro), chopped (reserve
    a few sprigs for garnish)
a handful dried egg noodles or
    capellini, broken into pieces
salt and ground black pepper
60–75ml/4–5 tbsp creamy yogurt,
    to serve

SERVES 4

street food

relaxed eating

Food sold and eaten on the streets of Morocco gives the towns and villages a terrific ambience. The souks, old medinas, tiny, narrow streets, busy boulevards, ports, bus and train stations are alive with food-centred activity. Street vendors sell their specialities from ramshackle stalls or from baskets and trays carried through the crowds.

Spicy snails, sweet hashish balls, aromatic breads and filled savoury pastries appear from nowhere. Donkeys and traders alike are bent over with their burdens, laden with sacks of grain, while vegetables arrive from the fields in horse- or donkey-drawn carts. Amongst the dust, slanting sunlight and long shadows, the scenes are almost medieval as well-covered women gather in groups to haggle and men splattered in dirt with lit cigarettes dangling from their mouths scurry about unpacking loads, setting up stalls and preparing food. The smell of fire, smoke and cooking fills the air and lingers long into the night.

At dawn, light and golden fritters are deep-fried in vast cauldrons and sold in sheets of paper. Also in the mornings, people gather in cafés to gulp down bowls of steaming chickpea and lentil soup – *harira* – or plates of thick, hot pancakes – *baghira* – dripping with honey. The enticing smell of freshly baked bread and rolls emanates from almost every corner and every stall, where people stop to buy a few aromatic buns or a wedge of a *cuajada*, a Spanish-style omelette. Dried fruit and nuts, spices and dried herbs are always on display ready to nibble or sprinkle over a snack. No matter what time of day or night, there is always something delicious to eat.

When travelling in Morocco, it is difficult to stop yourself eating. The cooking in the streets smells so good. The great thing is that most of it is fairly simple to cook at home for a snack or a meal. So, if you're feeling nostalgic from your last trip, create the taste of Moroccan street food in your home.

beghrir

These pancakes are smooth on one side, bubbly on the other and they melt in the mouth. Dripping with honey or drenched in sugar, they are often served for breakfast on cool, winter mornings in Morocco. They are also popular as a sweet snack in the streets. At home they are wonderful served with strawberry jam or, like blinis, with smoked salmon and sour cream.

Place the yeast in a small bowl and add 30ml/2 tbsp lukewarm water. Break up the yeast with a spoon and gradually press and stir it into the water until dissolved. Add a little extra water, if necessary, so that the yeast forms a thin, creamy paste. Cover the bowl and leave in a warm place for about 15 minutes, until frothy and bubbly.

Sift the semolina and flour with the salt into a large bowl. Make a well in the centre and drop in the eggs. Heat the milk and water together until just warm, then pour into the bowl, beating constantly. Pour in the yeast mixture and continue beating for 5 minutes. Cover the bowl with a cloth and leave the batter to rise in a warm place for at least 2 hours.

To cook the pancakes, heat a heavy frying pan and use a pad of kitchen paper to wipe it with a little oil. Pour a small cupful or ladleful of batter into the pan and spread evenly. Cook for about 2 minutes. Bubbles will form across the pancake and set in the batter. Lift out and wrap in a cloth to keep warm. Repeat with the remaining batter.

Melt the butter in a wide pan and dip the pancakes into it or, alternatively, pour the butter over them. Serve warm with clear honey.

Using dried yeast
If fresh yeast is not available, use 20g/¾oz easy-blend (rapid-rise) dried yeast. Mix this type of yeast with the semolina and flour before adding the liquids. Continue as in the main recipe.

40g/1½oz fresh yeast
400g/14oz/2¼ cups fine semolina
115g/4oz/1 cup plain
   (all-purpose) flour
5ml/1 tsp salt
3 eggs
300ml/½ pint/1¼ cups milk
900ml/1½ pints/3¾ cups water
oil, for frying
75g/3oz butter
clear honey, to serve

MAKES 20–30

kesra

Moroccan bread or other flat breads are the perfect accompaniment for all kinds of savoury dishes. Chunks of the warm, crusty loaves make wonderful scoops for tasty dips and are perfect for mopping up all the aromatic oils and cooking juices from salads and tagines. If you are short of time, you could use focaccia or ciabatta bread as an alternative.

sunflower or vegetable oil
75g/3oz/¾ cup corn meal
2.5ml/½ tsp dried yeast
scant 5ml/1 tsp sugar
600ml/1 pint/2½ cups
    lukewarm water
450g/1lb/4 cups unbleached
    strong white bread flour
5ml/1 tsp salt
30ml/2 tbsp melted butter
sesame seeds, to sprinkle

MAKES 2 ROUND LOAVES

Lightly oil two baking sheets and dust them with 15ml/1 tbsp of the corn meal. In a small bowl, dissolve the yeast and sugar in about 50ml/2fl oz/¼ cup of the lukewarm water. Sift the flour, the remaining corn meal and the salt into a bowl. Make a well in the centre and pour in the yeast mixture and the melted butter. Gradually add the remaining water, while using your hand to draw in the flour from the sides of the bowl and mix the ingredients into a dough. Add a little more flour if the dough becomes too sticky.

Knead the dough on a floured surface for about 10 minutes until smooth and elastic. Divide the dough in half and knead each piece into a ball. Flatten and stretch the balls of dough into circles, about 20cm/8in in diameter. Place on the baking sheets and sprinkle with sesame seeds. Cover the loaves with damp cloths and leave in a warm place for about 1 hour, until doubled in size.

Preheat the oven to 220°C/425°F/Gas 7. Pinch the tops of the loaves with your fingers or prick them with a fork. Bake for about 15 minutes, then reduce the oven temperature to 180°C/350°F/Gas 4 and bake for a further 15 minutes, or until the loaves are crusty, golden and sound hollow when tapped underneath. Cool on a wire rack.

Shaping and flavouring the bread
The dough can be shaped in any way you prefer or made into individual rolls. For ceremonial occasions, aniseed or fennel seeds are added to flavour the bread. To make a delicious breakfast bread, use half and half wholemeal (whole-wheat) and white flours and add a little honey to the dough with the lukewarm water.

bruschetta with anchovies, quail's eggs and roasted cumin

All over the Middle East and North Africa, hard-boiled eggs are enjoyed as a snack or appetizer, dipped in salt and paprika; in the thyme and sumac mixture, zahtar; or in roasted cumin. Bitesize quail's eggs dipped in warm and aromatic, freshly roasted cumin are my favourite – they are great for picnics or they marry well with anchovies to make this tasty bruschetta.

Preheat the grill (broiler) on the hottest setting. Slice the loaf of bread horizontally in half and toast the cut side until golden. Smash the garlic cloves with the flat blade of a knife to remove their skins and crush the flesh slightly, and rub them over the toasted bread. Drizzle the olive oil over the bread and sprinkle with a little salt (not too much as the anchovies will be salty).

Cut each length of bread into four to six equal pieces. Pile the onion slices, quail's egg halves and anchovy fillets on the pieces of bread. Sprinkle liberally with the ground roasted cumin and chopped parsley and serve immediately while the bread is still warm.

Choosing and preparing anchovy fillets
Select anchovy fillets preserved in salt or oil. Soak anchovy fillets preserved in salt in a little milk for about 15 minutes to reduce the salty flavour, then drain (discarding the milk) and pat dry on kitchen paper. Drain fillets preserved in oil.

1 Moroccan or ciabatta loaf
2–3 garlic cloves
30–45ml/2–3 tbsp olive oil
1 red onion, halved and
    finely sliced
12 quail's eggs, boiled for about
    4 minutes, shelled and halved
50g/2oz anchovy fillets
10–15ml/2–3 tsp cumin seeds,
    roasted and ground
small bunch of flat leaf parsley,
    roughly chopped
coarse salt

SERVES 4–6

savoury cigars and triangles

Known as *briouats* in Morocco, these little savoury pastries are filled with minced lamb or beef, spinach or cheese with herbs. Easy to make, they are always shaped into cigars or triangles and the fillings can be varied to suit individual tastes. The fillings can be prepared ahead of time but the pastry should only be unwrapped when you are ready to make the pastries, otherwise it will dry out.

Prepare the fillings. To make the feta cheese filling, place the cheese in a bowl and mash with a fork, then beat in the eggs and chopped herbs.

To make the beef filling, heat the olive oil in a heavy frying pan. Add the onion and pine nuts; cook, stirring, until coloured, then stir in the ras el hanout. Add the beef and cook for about 15 minutes, stirring, until browned. Season and cool.

To make the spinach filling, melt the butter in a small heavy pan. Add the onion and cook over a low heat for 15 minutes until softened. Stir in the spinach and coriander. Season with nutmeg, salt and pepper, then cool.

Lay a sheet of ouarka or filo pastry on a work surface. Cut the sheet widthways into four strips. Spoon a little filling mixture on the first strip, at the end nearest to you. Fold the corners of the pastry over the mixture to seal it, then roll up the pastry and filling away from you into a tight cigar. As you reach the end of the strip, brush the edges with a little water and continue to roll up the cigar to seal in the filling. Repeat, placing the finished cigars under a damp cloth.

Heat the sunflower oil for deep-frying to 180°C/350°F, or until a cube of day-old bread browns in 30–45 seconds. Add the cigars to the oil in batches and fry over a medium heat until golden brown. Drain on kitchen paper and serve warm.

8 sheets of ouarka or filo pastry
sunflower oil, for deep-frying

FOR THE FETA CHEESE FILLING
450g/1lb feta cheese
4 eggs
bunch of fresh coriander
    (cilantro), finely chopped
bunch of flat leaf parsley,
    finely chopped
bunch of mint, finely chopped

FOR THE BEEF FILLING
15–30ml/1–2 tbsp olive oil
1 onion, finely chopped
30ml/2 tbsp pine nuts
5ml/1 tsp ras el hanout
225g/8oz minced (ground) beef
salt and ground black pepper

FOR THE SPINACH FILLING
50g/2oz/¼ cup butter
1 onion, finely chopped
275g/10oz fresh spinach, cooked,
    drained and chopped
small bunch of fresh coriander
    (cilantro), finely chopped
pinch of grated nutmeg
salt and ground black pepper

MAKES ABOUT 32

sesame-coated majoun

You will find these sweet, spicy fruit and nut balls on every street corner in Morocco. The quantity of spices varies from cook to cook, and the secret to their delicious flavour is often in the amount of hashish used. For these are the infamous hashish balls, popular as a narcotic or as an aphrodisiac; however in this version the hashish is omitted (with some detriment to flavour!).

Finely chop the almonds, walnuts and raisins in a food processor or blender until they form a coarse, slightly sticky mixture. Alternatively, pound these ingredients together in batches in a large mortar using a pestle until the correct consistency is reached – you will need to do this in batches.

Melt the butter in a large heavy pan and stir in the honey, ras el hanout and ginger. Add the nuts and raisins and stir over a gentle heat for a few seconds until the mixture is thoroughly combined, firm and sticky. Cool a little, then shape into about 20 balls. Roll the balls in sesame seeds to coat completely.

500g/1¼lb blanched almonds
250g/9oz/1½ cups walnuts
500g/1¼lb raisins
250g/9oz/generous 1 cup
   clear honey
130g/4½oz/generous ½ cup butter
7.5ml/1½ tsp ras el hanout
7.5ml/1½ tsp ground ginger
60–75g/4–5oz sesame seeds

MAKES ABOUT 20

spicy plantain snacks

Sweet and crisp, deep-fried slices of plantain are not only a great street snack, but they also make excellent nibbles with drinks. Make sure the plantains are ripe – the skin should be brown and mottled – otherwise they tend to be woody rather than sweet and fruity. Be liberal with the spices as the starchy plantains are able to carry strong flavours.

2 large ripe plantains
sunflower oil, for deep-frying
1 dried red chilli, roasted,
    seeded and chopped
15–30ml/1–2 tbsp zhatar
coarse salt

SERVES 2–4 AS A SNACK

To peel the plantains, cut off their ends with a sharp knife and make two to three incisions in the skin from end to end, then peel off the skin. Cut the plantains into thick slices.

Heat the oil for deep-frying to 180°C/350°F, or until a cube of day-old bread browns in 30–45 seconds. Fry the plantain slices in batches until golden brown. Drain each batch on a double layer of kitchen paper.

While still warm, place them in a shallow bowl and sprinkle liberally with the dried chilli, zahtar and salt. Toss them thoroughly and eat immediately.

Roasting the chilli
Place the chilli in a small, heavy frying pan and cook over a medium heat, stirring constantly, until the chilli darkens and gives off a peppery aroma.

picnic pie with egg, cashew nuts, ginger and coriander

This is a homely version of the more elaborate and traditional *bastilla*. Any mixture of nuts and herbs can be used, but the cashew nuts make this recipe more unusual. Served with a fruity Moroccan salad, such as artichoke heart and orange salad or grapefruit and fennel salad, this pie makes a delightful meal or, on a lovely summer day, it is great to take on a picnic.

30ml/2 tbsp olive oil
115g/4oz/½ cup butter
8 spring onions (scallions),
    trimmed and chopped
2 garlic cloves, chopped
25g/1oz fresh root ginger, peeled
    and chopped
225g/8oz/2 cups cashew nuts,
    roughly chopped
5–10ml/1–2 tsp ground
    cinnamon, plus extra to garnish
5ml/1 tsp paprika
2.5ml/½ tsp ground coriander,
    plus extra for dusting
6 eggs, beaten
bunch of flat leaf parsley,
    finely chopped
large bunch of fresh coriander
    (cilantro), finely chopped
8 sheets of ouarka or filo pastry
salt and ground black pepper

SERVES 6

Preheat the oven to 200°C/400°F/Gas 6. Heat the olive oil with a little of the butter in a heavy pan and stir in the spring onions, garlic and ginger. Add the cashew nuts and cook for a few minutes, then stir in the cinnamon, paprika and ground coriander. Season well, then add the eggs. Cook, stirring constantly, until the eggs begin to scramble but remain moist. Remove the pan from the heat, add the parsley and fresh coriander, and leave to cool.

Melt the remaining butter. Separate the sheets of ouarka or filo and keep them under a slightly damp cloth. Brush the base of an ovenproof dish with a little of the melted butter and cover with a sheet of pastry, allowing the sides to flop over the rim. Brush the pastry with a little more of the melted butter and place another sheet of pastry on top. Repeat with another two sheets of pastry to make four layers.

Spread the cashew nut mixture on the pastry and fold the pastry edges over the filling. Cover with the remaining sheets of pastry, brushing each one with melted butter and tucking the edges under the pie, as though you were making a bed.

Brush the top of the pie with the remaining melted butter and bake for 25 minutes, or until the pastry is crisp and golden. Dust the top of the pie with a little extra ground cinnamon and then serve immediately.

Making individual pies
Instead of making a single large pie, you can make small, individual pies for a picnic or to serve with drinks at a party. Simply cut the filo into strips or triangles, add a spoonful of the filling and fold them up into tight little parcels, making sure the edges are well sealed.

fish and chermoula mini pies

These little savoury pies are made with the Moroccan fine pastry ouarka, but filo pastry will work just as well. The filling is highly flavoured with chermoula, which is a mixture of spices and masses of fresh coriander and flat leaf parsley. The chermoula may be made in advance and stored in the refrigerator for a few days. You can vary the filling by adding mussels or scallops, if you like.

Prepare the chermoula. Combine all the ingredients in a bowl and set aside. Place the fish in a frying pan and add just enough water to cover the fillets. Season with a little salt and heat until just simmering, then cook gently for 3 minutes, or until the fish just begins to flake. Use a slotted spoon to remove the fish from the liquid and break it up, taking care to remove all bones.

Poach the prawns in the fish liquor for 10 minutes, until they turn pink, then drain and shell them. Gently toss the prawns and fish in the chermoula, cover and set aside for 1 hour.

Preheat the oven to 180°C/350°F/Gas 4 and grease two baking sheets. To make the pies, open out the sheets of filo pastry but keep them under a damp cloth. Take two sheets of pastry: brush a sheet with oil and lay the second one on top, then brush it with a little oil. Place some of the fish mixture in the middle of the length of the sheet but to one side of its width. Fold the edge of the pastry over the filling, then fold the long side over to cover the filling completely. Wrap the ends of the pastry around the filling like a collar to make a neat package with the edges tucked in, then brush with egg yolk. Continue in the same way with the rest of the filo and chermoula mixture, then bake the pies for about 20 minutes until the pastry is golden brown.

Making triangular or open pies
Instead of neat parcels, the filo and filling can be folded into triangles, or shaped into open boats or slipper shapes.

500g/1¼lb firm white fish fillets
225g/8oz uncooked king prawns
  (jumbo shrimp)
16 sheets of ouarka or filo pastry
60–75ml/4–5 tbsp sunflower oil
1 egg yolk, mixed with a few
  drops of water
salt

FOR THE CHERMOULA
75ml/5 tbsp olive oil
juice of 1 lemon
5ml/1 tsp ground cumin
5–10ml/1–2 tsp paprika
2–3 garlic cloves, crushed
1 red chilli, seeded and chopped
large bunch of flat leaf
  parsley, chopped
large bunch of fresh coriander
  (cilantro), chopped

MAKES 8

roast chicken with cucumber and tomato salad in pitta pockets

Cucumber and tomato salads are so simple yet hugely versatile. Add them to mezze spreads for their refreshing flavour and crunchy texture; offer as a palate cleanser during a feast of several courses; or tuck into pitta and flat bread wraps for a snack. The chicken in these pitta breads can be hot or cold – either roast a small bird specially or use up the leftovers from a large roast chicken.

Place the cucumber in a strainer over a bowl, sprinkle with a little salt and leave for 10 minutes to drain. Rinse well and drain again, then place in a bowl with the tomatoes and spring onions. Stir in the olive oil, parsley, mint and preserved lemon. Season well.

In a small bowl, mix the tahini with the lemon juice, then thin the mixture down with a little water to the consistency of thick double (heavy) cream. Beat in the garlic and season.

Preheat the grill (broiler) to hot. Lightly toast the pitta breads well away from the heat source until they puff up. (Alternatively, lightly toast the breads in a toaster.) Open the breads and stuff them liberally with the chicken and salad. Drizzle a generous amount of tahini sauce into each one and serve immediately.

Tahini
This thick, creamy sesame paste is enjoyed throughout North Africa and the Middle East. There are two types of tahini – light and dark. The lighter one is superior in flavour and texture.

1 small cucumber, peeled
  and diced
3 tomatoes, peeled, seeded
  and chopped
2 spring onions
  (scallions), chopped
30ml/2 tbsp olive oil
small bunch of flat leaf parsley,
  finely chopped
small bunch of mint,
  finely chopped
½ preserved lemon,
  finely chopped
45–60ml/3–4 tbsp tahini
juice of 1 lemon
2 garlic cloves, crushed
6 pitta breads
½ small roast chicken or 2 large
  roast chicken breasts, cut
  into strips
salt and ground black pepper

MAKES 6

spring rolls with chicken, spring onions and almonds

The classic pigeon *bistilla* is Morocco's most famous dish. It is an exquisite pastry with two savoury layers and one sweet layer flavoured with cinnamon. Traditionally, the *bistilla* is always served to commence a *diffa*, a ceremonial feast of many courses, and is eaten by tearing bits off with the fingers. This is a street-style spring roll version, which is easy to eat and delicious dipped in a sweet mixture of ground almonds and cinnamon.

To make the filling, place the chicken in a large pan and cover with water. Add the onion, garlic, butter, cinnamon, ginger, ras el hanout, saffron, half the parsley and half the coriander. Bring to the boil, then reduce the heat, cover and simmer for about 1 hour, until the chicken is cooked through and tender.

Lift the chicken out of the pan and set aside to cool. Boil the cooking liquid until it is reduced to 550ml/18fl oz/2½ cups. Season with salt and pepper and remove from the heat. Pour the beaten eggs into the hot stock, stirring until the egg has set, then drain through a fine strainer.

Cut the meat off the chicken and shred coarsely. Place in a bowl; add the egg with the remaining parsley and coriander, the orange flower water, lemon juice and spring onions. Mix well. In another bowl, combine the dipping ingredients.

In a bowl, mix together the flour with the water to form a paste. Place a spring roll wrapper on a work surface with one corner facing you. (Keep the others under a damp dishtowel.) Sprinkle some almond dipping mixture over the wrapper. Place a tablespoon of the chicken mixture in a line 5cm/2in in from the corner. Fold the corner over the filling and roll it slightly. Fold in the sides so they overlap and enclose the filling. Roll up the spring roll tightly, holding the sides, then seal the end with a little flour paste. Repeat with the remaining wrappers and filling.

Heat the sunflower oil for deep-frying to 180°C/350°F, or until a cube of day-old bread browns in 30–45 seconds. Cook the spring rolls three or four at a time until crisp and golden. Drain on kitchen paper and serve immediately with the almond mixture for dipping.

30ml/2 tbsp plain
  (all-purpose) flour
about 30ml/2 tbsp water
12 large spring roll wrappers
sunflower oil, for deep-frying

FOR THE FILLING
1 small chicken
½ onion, finely chopped
3–4 garlic cloves, finely chopped
25g/1oz/2 tbsp butter
1 cinnamon stick
5ml/1 tsp ground ginger
5ml/1 tsp ras el hanout
pinch of saffron threads
small bunch of flat leaf
  parsley, chopped
small bunch of fresh coriander
  (cilantro), chopped
6 eggs, beaten
10ml/2 tsp orange flower water
½ lemon
6–8 spring onions (scallions),
  thickly sliced
salt and ground black pepper

FOR THE DIPPING MIXTURE
115g/4oz/1 cup blanched
  almonds, lightly toasted
  and coarsely ground
30ml/2 tbsp icing
  (confectioners') sugar
5–10ml/1–2 tsp ground cinnamon

SERVES 6

bus-station kefta
with egg and tomato

Egg and tomato dishes are very popular in bus and train stations and ports around the Middle East and North Africa. Travellers waiting for connecting transport services tuck into dishes like this to sustain themselves during long journeys. The dish is always eaten out of the pan in which it is cooked. It would make a great informal brunch or supper dish.

225g/8oz finely minced
    (ground) lamb
1 onion, finely chopped
50g/2oz fresh breadcrumbs
5 eggs
5ml/1 tsp ground cinnamon
small bunch of flat leaf parsley,
    finely chopped
30ml/2 tbsp olive oil
a little butter
400g/14oz can chopped tomatoes
10ml/2 tsp sugar
5ml/1 tsp ras el hanout
small bunch of fresh coriander
    (cilantro), roughly chopped
salt and ground black pepper
crusty bread, to serve

SERVES 4

In a bowl, knead the minced lamb with the onion, breadcrumbs, 1 egg, cinnamon, parsley and salt and pepper until well mixed. Lift the mixture in your hand and slap it down into the bowl several times. Take a small amount of mixture and shape it into a small ball about the size of a walnut. Repeat with the remaining mixture to make about 12 balls.

Heat the olive oil with the butter in a large heavy frying pan. Fry the meatballs until nicely browned, turning them occasionally so they cook evenly. Stir in the tomatoes, sugar, ras el hanout and most of the coriander. Bring to the boil, cook for a few minutes to reduce the liquid, and roll the balls in the sauce. Season to taste with salt and pepper.

Make room for the remaining eggs in the pan and crack them into spaces between the meatballs. Cover the pan, reduce the heat and cook for about 3 minutes or until the eggs are just set. Sprinkle with the remaining coriander and serve in the pan, with chunks of bread to use as scoops.

couscous & tagines

a traditional combination

The preparation of tagines and couscous – known as *seksou* by the indigenous Berbers – are among the oldest, most traditional methods of cooking in Morocco today. A tagine is a highly flavoured stew, usually meat based, cooked slowly over charcoal in a special earthenware dish with a conical lid, which is also called a tagine, designed to allow the food to cook in its own steam.

In the seventh century when Arab soldiers settled in the region, they introduced spices such as cinnamon, ginger, caraway and cumin that were quickly included in the traditional tagines. They also introduced the idea of matching sweet with sour, using honey and fruit. It is this sweet and sour taste, combined with warm aromatic spices, that gives the Moroccan tagines their own distinct character.

Classic tagines include lamb with prunes and almonds, fish with tomatoes, ginger and saffron, and chicken with olives and preserved lemon, and it is these combinations that influence the modern versions and variations in the recipes in this chapter. *Qamama* tagines, which are made with onions, are regarded as superior and great praise is heaped on the cook if the tagine is golden and caramelized. Another type of tagine known as a *kdra* is cooked in the aged butter, *smen*, the preferred cooking fat of the Berbers, which adds its distinctive flavour to the tagine.

The secret of a good tagine is to simmer the meat until it is very tender, allowing the oil or butter to mingle with the liquid to produce a velvety sauce, which must be served piping hot. This combination of rich, sweet and spicy flavours in a thick sauce can be unbelievably delicious. The liquor is best mopped up with chunks of bread. Traditionally, the tagine would just be one of many courses in a meal and served with a salad or bread but it can be served with couscous or rice to turn it into a meal in itself.

Couscous is recognized as the signature dish of Maghrebi cuisine, originally created by the Berbers using durum wheat introduced by the Carthaginians. Traditionally, Moroccans put a lot of effort into making couscous, washing and soaking it, aerating it by hand in a *g'saa* – a large, round wooden or earthenware bowl – and then alternating the steaming and aerating with a little oil or butter. The familiar commercial varieties that are available today tend to be pre-cooked or instant, making preparation easier as once the grain has absorbed an equal volume of water it simply needs to be steamed until heated through.

In most Moroccan households, couscous is served as a course on its own, presented at the end of a long meal by a host anxious to ensure that guests do not depart with even the tiniest hole unfilled. Sometimes, a lavish dish of couscous may be prepared for the family meal and served in a mound with a loose stew spooned around the base and the broth poured over the top. Like everything else, couscous is eaten with the fingers of the right hand. The knack is to pick out a chickpea, nut or raisin with a fingerful of the cooked grain, then press it carefully into a small ball and, with a twist of the thumb, pop it into the mouth. If there is a lot of sauce or broth with the couscous, a little bowl of perfumed water is provided to clean the fingers at the end of the meal. At home, you might prefer to use a fork. Couscous is also wonderful served with a tasty tagine. Combined, they make an excellent meal.

casablancan couscous
with roasted summer vegetables

This dish is based on the classic couscous recipe for a stew containing seven vegetables. The number seven is believed to bring good luck, so you can use vegetables of your choice as long as they add up to seven in type. I like to serve this dish with a dollop of thick and creamy yogurt but, if you wish, you can also serve it with a spoonful of fiery harissa as a condiment.

Preheat the oven to 200°C/400°F/Gas 6. Arrange all the vegetables in a roasting pan. Tuck the garlic, ginger and rosemary around the vegetables. Pour lots of olive oil over the vegetables, sprinkle with the sugar or honey, salt and pepper, and roast for about 1½ hours until they are extremely tender and slightly caramelized. The cooking time will depend on the size of the vegetable pieces. Turn them in the oil occasionally.

When the vegetables are nearly ready, put the couscous in a bowl. Stir the salt into the water, then pour it over the couscous, stirring to make sure it is absorbed evenly. Leave to stand for 10 minutes to plump up then, using your fingers, rub the sunflower oil into the grains to air them and break up any lumps. Tip the couscous into an ovenproof dish, arrange the butter over the top, cover with foil and heat in the oven for about 20 minutes.

To serve, use your fingers to work the melted butter into the grains of couscous and fluff it up, then pile it on a large dish and shape into a mound with a little pit at the top. Spoon some vegetables into the pit and arrange the rest around the dish. Pour the oil from the pan over the couscous or serve separately. Serve immediately with yogurt, or harissa if you prefer, and bread for mopping up the juices.

3 red onions, peeled and
  quartered
2–3 courgettes (zucchini), halved
  lengthways and cut across into
  2–3 pieces
2–3 red, green or yellow (bell)
  peppers, seeded and quartered
2 aubergines (eggplant), cut into
  6–8 long segments
2–3 leeks, trimmed and cut into
  long strips
2–3 sweet potatoes, peeled,
  halved lengthways and cut
  into long strips
4–6 tomatoes, quartered
6 garlic cloves, crushed
25g/1oz fresh root ginger, sliced
a few large fresh rosemary sprigs
about 150ml/¼ pint/⅔ cup olive oil
10ml/2 tsp sugar or clear honey
salt and ground black pepper
natural (plain) yogurt or harissa
  and bread, to serve

FOR THE COUSCOUS
500g/1¼lb/3 cups medium
  couscous
5ml/1 tsp salt
600ml/1 pint/2½ cups warm water
45ml/3 tbsp sunflower oil
about 25g/1oz/2 tbsp butter, diced

SERVES 6

spicy couscous
with aromatic shellfish broth

Some couscous dishes include a soup-like stew, which is ladled over the cooked couscous and mopped up with lots of bread. In this recipe, mussels and prawns have been used but you could use any shellfish, either shelled or in their shells. This is the type of dish you can enjoy on a warm evening along the coast by Casablanca or Tangier.

Preheat the oven to 180°C/350°F/Gas 4. Place the couscous in a bowl. Stir the salt into the water, then pour over the couscous, stirring. Set aside for 10 minutes.

Stir the sunflower oil into the harissa to make a paste, then, using your fingers, rub it into the couscous and break up any lumps. Tip into an ovenproof dish, arrange the butter over, cover with foil and heat in the oven for about 20 minutes.

Meanwhile, put the mussels and prawns in a pan, add the lemon juice and 50ml/2fl oz/¼ cup water, cover and cook for 3–4 minutes, shaking the pan, until the mussels have opened. Drain the shellfish, reserving the liquor, and shell about two-thirds of the mussels and prawns. Discard any closed mussels.

Heat the butter in a large pan. Cook the shallots for 5 minutes, or until softened. Add the spices and fry for 1 minute. Off the heat, stir in the flour, the fish stock and shellfish cooking liquor. Bring to the boil, stirring. Add the cream and simmer, stirring occasionally, for about 10 minutes. Season with salt and pepper, add the shellfish and most of the fresh coriander. Heat through, then sprinkle with the remaining coriander.

Fluff up the couscous with a fork or your fingers, working in the melted butter. To serve, pass round the couscous and ladle the broth over the top.

Roasting spices
Toss the spices in a heavy pan over a high heat until they begin to change colour and give off a nutty aroma, then immediately tip them into a bowl.

500g/1¼lb/3 cups medium
  couscous
5ml/1 tsp salt
600ml/1 pint/2½ cups warm water
45ml/3 tbsp sunflower oil
5–10ml/1–2 tsp harissa
25g/1oz/2 tbsp butter, diced

FOR THE SHELLFISH BROTH
500g/1¼lb mussels in their shells,
  scrubbed with beards removed
500g/1¼lb uncooked prawns
  (shrimp) in their shells
juice of 1 lemon
50g/2oz/2 tbsp butter
2 shallots, finely chopped
5ml/1 tsp coriander seeds, roasted
  and ground
5ml/1 tsp cumin seeds, roasted
  and ground
2.5ml/½ tsp ground turmeric
2.5ml/½ tsp cayenne pepper
5–10ml/1–2 tsp plain
  (all-purpose) flour
600ml/1 pint/2½ cups fish stock
120ml/4fl oz/½ cup double
  (heavy) cream
salt and ground black pepper
small bunch of fresh coriander
  (cilantro), finely chopped,
  to serve

SERVES 4–6

couscous with lamb cutlets, harissa and fennel

This style of couscous dish is often served with sour pickles, such as cabbage or hot peppers. Throughout the Middle East and North Africa, every butcher prepares thin lamb cutlets for grilling or frying – ask your butcher to do the same for this dish.

Heat the olive oil in a heavy pan, add the onions and garlic and cook for 15 minutes, until softened. Mix the tomato purée with the harissa and dilute with a little water. Pour it into the pan with 600ml/1 pint/2½ cups water. Bring to the boil and add the fennel. Reduce the heat, cover and cook for about 10 minutes, or until tender.

Meanwhile, prepare the couscous. Stir the salt into the water. Place the couscous in a bowl and cover with the water, stirring. Set aside for 10 minutes. Using your fingers, rub the sunflower oil into the couscous. Use a slotted spoon to lift the vegetables from the cooking liquid and transfer to a covered dish; keep warm.

Bring the liquid to the boil to reduce it. Melt the butter in a heavy frying pan, add the cutlets to the pan and brown them on both sides. Add the cutlets to the reduced liquid and simmer for 15 minutes, or until tender.

Preheat the oven to 180°C/350°F/Gas 4. Tip the couscous into an ovenproof dish and arrange the diced butter over the top. Chop the fennel fronds and sprinkle over the couscous. Cover with foil and heat in the oven for about 20 minutes.

Put the vegetables in the pan with the lamb and heat through. Fluff up the couscous then mound it on to a serving dish. Place the cutlets around the edge and spoon the vegetables over. Moisten with the cooking liquid and serve.

Making pickled vegetables

Crunchy pickles make a delicious accompaniment to serve with this dish and are easy to make. Simply combine whole or chopped raw vegetables with white wine vinegar mixed with a little salt and leave to soak for about 3 weeks. The most popular pickled vegetables enjoyed in Morocco are green tomatoes, hot peppers, white cabbage and garlic.

45ml/3 tbsp olive oil
2 onions, quartered
4 garlic cloves, chopped
30–45ml/2–3 tbsp tomato
  purée (paste)
10ml/2 tsp harissa
4 fennel bulbs, stalks removed
  and quartered (feathery
  fronds reserved)
50g/2oz/¼ cup butter
8 thin lamb cutlets (US rib chops)
salt and ground black pepper

FOR THE COUSCOUS
2.5ml/½ tsp salt
400ml/14fl oz/1⅔ cups warm
  water
350g/12oz/2 cups medium
  couscous
30ml/2 tbsp sunflower oil
knob (pat) of butter, diced

SERVES 4

tagine of artichoke hearts, potatoes, peas and saffron

When artichokes are in season, this succulent tagine is a favourite country dish made using other produce from the garden or fields as well. Fresh coriander, parsley and mint combine to complement the summery flavours of the vegetables while turmeric contributes its earthy warmth. Prepare the artichokes yourself by removing the outer leaves, cutting off the stems, and scooping out the choke and hairy bits with a teaspoon, or buy frozen prepared hearts.

Poach the artichoke hearts very gently in plenty of simmering water with half the lemon juice, for 10–15 minutes until tender. Drain and refresh under cold running water, then drain again.

Heat the olive oil in a tagine or heavy pan. Add the chopped onion and cook over a low heat for about 15 minutes, or until softened but not browned. Add the potatoes, most of the parsley, the coriander, mint, the remaining lemon juice, and the saffron and turmeric to the pan. Pour in the vegetable stock, bring to the boil, then reduce the heat. Cover the pan and cook for about 15 minutes, or until the potatoes are almost tender.

Stir the preserved lemon, artichoke hearts and peas into the stew, and cook, uncovered, for a further 10 minutes. Season to taste, sprinkle with the remaining parsley, and serve with couscous or chunks of fresh bread.

Preparing artichokes
Once cut, the flesh of artichokes will blacken. To prevent this from happening, put the artichokes into acidulated water – you can use lemon juice or white wine vinegar.

6 fresh artichoke hearts
juice of 1 lemon
30–45ml/2–3 tbsp olive oil
1 onion, chopped
675g/1½lb potatoes, peeled
    and quartered
small bunch of flat leaf
    parsley, chopped
small bunch of coriander
    (cilantro), chopped
small bunch of mint, chopped
pinch of saffron threads
5ml/1 tsp ground turmeric
about 350ml/12fl oz/1½ cups
    vegetable stock
finely chopped rind of
    ½ preserved lemon
250g/9oz/2¼ cups shelled peas
salt and ground black pepper
couscous or bread, to serve

SERVES 4–6

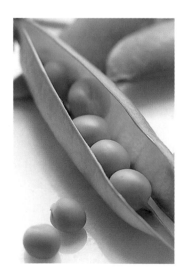

tagine of monkfish, potatoes, cherry tomatoes and olives

The fish for this tagine is marinated in chermoula, which gives it that unmistakable Moroccan flavour. It is a delightful dish at any time of year, served with lots of crusty bread to mop up the tasty juices, but it is especially good made with full-flavoured, new season potatoes and little sun-ripened cherry tomatoes.

Using a mortar and pestle to make the chermoula: pound the garlic with the salt to a smooth paste. Add the cumin, paprika, lemon juice and coriander, and gradually mix in the olive oil to emulsify the mixture slightly. Reserve a little chermoula for cooking, then rub the rest of the paste over the chunks of monkfish. Cover and leave to marinate for about 1 hour.

Par-boil the potatoes for about 10 minutes until slightly softened. Drain, refresh under cold water and drain again, then cut them in half lengthways. Heat the olive oil in a heavy pan and stir in the garlic. When the garlic begins to colour, add the tomatoes and cook until just softened. Add the peppers and the remaining chermoula, and season with salt and pepper.

Spread the potatoes over the base of a tagine, shallow pan or deep, ridged frying pan. Spoon three-quarters of the tomato and pepper mixture over and place the marinated fish chunks on top, with their marinade. Spoon the rest of the tomato and pepper mixture on top of the fish and add the olives. Drizzle a little extra olive oil over the dish and pour in the water. Heat until simmering, cover the tagine or pan with a lid and steam over a medium heat for about 15 minutes, or until the fish is cooked through. Serve with fresh, warm crusty bread to mop up the delicious juices.

900g/2lb monkfish tail, cut
   into chunks
15–20 small new potatoes,
   scrubbed, scraped or peeled
45–60ml/3–4 tbsp olive oil
4–5 garlic cloves, thinly sliced
15–20 cherry tomatoes
2 green (bell) peppers, grilled
   (broiled) until black, skinned,
   seeded and cut into strips
large handful of kalamata or
   fleshy black olives
about 100ml/3½fl oz/
   scant ½ cup water
salt and ground black pepper

FOR THE CHERMOULA
2 garlic cloves
5ml/1 tsp coarse salt
10ml/2 tsp ground cumin
5ml/1 tsp paprika
juice of 1 lemon
small bunch of fresh coriander
   (cilantro), roughly chopped
15ml/1 tbsp olive oil

SERVES 4

chicken tagine with green olives and preserved lemon

This dish, which is particularly enjoyed in Marrakesh, celebrates two of Morocco's most famous ingredients – cracked green olives and preserved lemons. Try this recipe when you are looking for a new way to cook a whole chicken instead of by the usual roasting method. Serve simply with plain couscous and a salad or vegetable side dish.

Place the chicken in a deep dish. Rub the garlic, coriander, lemon juice and salt into the body cavity of the chicken. Mix the olive oil with the grated onion, saffron, ginger and pepper and rub this mixture over the outside of the chicken. Cover and leave to stand for about 30 minutes.

Transfer the chicken to a tagine or large, heavy flameproof casserole and pour the marinating juices over. Pour in enough water to come halfway up the chicken, add the cinnamon stick and bring the water to the boil. Reduce the heat, cover with a lid and simmer for about 1 hour, turning the chicken occasionally.

Preheat the oven to 150°C/300°F/Gas 2. Using two slotted spoons, carefully lift the chicken out of the tagine or casserole and set aside on a plate, covered with foil. Turn up the heat and boil the cooking liquid for 5 minutes to reduce it. Replace the chicken in the liquid and baste it thoroughly. Add the olives and preserved lemon and place the tagine or casserole in the oven for about 15 minutes. Serve the chicken immediately with your chosen accompaniments.

1.3kg/3lb chicken
3 garlic cloves, crushed
small bunch of fresh coriander
   (cilantro), finely chopped
juice of ½ lemon
5ml/1 tsp coarse salt
45–60ml/3–4 tbsp olive oil
1 large onion, grated
pinch of saffron threads
5ml/1 tsp ground ginger
5ml/1 tsp ground black pepper
1 cinnamon stick
175g/6oz/1½ cups cracked
   green olives
2 preserved lemons, cut into strips

SERVES 4

tagine of poussins with dates and orange flower water

Dates and almonds are probably the most ancient culinary combination in Arab cuisines, married in sweet dishes or with lamb and chicken. For this type of tagine, the small birds can be cooked on top of the stove or in the oven. Quail, partridge, pheasant or pigeon can be used instead of poussins, if you like. Served with a Moroccan salad and couscous, this makes a lovely dinner party dish.

25g/1oz fresh root ginger, peeled and roughly chopped
2 garlic cloves
60ml/4 tbsp olive oil
juice of 1 lemon
30–45ml/2–3 tbsp clear honey
4 small poussins
350g/12oz/2 cups moist dried dates, pitted
5–10ml/1–2 tsp ground cinnamon
15ml/1 tbsp orange flower water
30–45ml/2–3 tbsp blanched almonds
knob of butter
salt and ground black pepper

SERVES 4

Using a mortar and pestle, crush the ginger with the garlic to form a paste. Mix the paste with the olive oil, lemon juice, honey and seasoning.

Place the poussins in a tagine or flameproof casserole and rub the paste all over them. Pour in a little water to cover the base of the dish and bring to the boil. Reduce the heat, cover and simmer for about 30 minutes, turning the poussins occasionally, until they are cooked through. Top up the water during cooking, if necessary.

Lift the poussins out of the tagine, transfer them to a plate, cover with foil and keep hot. Add the dates to the liquid in the tagine and stir in the cinnamon and orange flower water. Cook gently for about 10 minutes, or until the dates are soft and have absorbed the flavours of the sauce as well as some of the liquid.

Replace the poussins and cover the tagine to keep hot. Melt the butter in a separate pan and brown the almonds, then toss them over the poussins. Serve immediately.

tagine of spiced kefta
with lemon and spices

The kefta, or meatballs, are poached gently with lemon and spices to make a dish that is quite light and ideal for lunch. Serve it with a salad or plain couscous. In Morocco today, this dish has no boundaries. It can be found in the tiniest rural villages, in street stalls in the towns and cities, or in the finest restaurants of Casablanca, Fez and Marakesh.

To make the kefta, pound the minced lamb in a bowl by using your hand to lift it up and slap it back down into the bowl. Knead in half the grated onions, the parsley, cinnamon, cumin and cayenne pepper. Season with salt and pepper, and continue pounding the mixture by hand for a few minutes. Break off pieces of the mixture and shape them into walnut-size balls.

In a heavy lidded frying pan, melt the butter and add the remaining onion with the ginger, chilli and saffron. Stirring frequently, cook just until the onion begins to colour, then stir in the coriander and lemon juice.

Pour in the water, season with salt and bring to the boil. Drop in the kefta, reduce the heat and cover the pan. Poach the kefta gently, turning them occasionally, for about 20 minutes.

Remove the lid, tuck the lemon quarters around the kefta and cook, uncovered, for a further 10 minutes to reduce the liquid slightly. Serve hot, straight from the pan with lots of crusty fresh bread to mop up the delicious juices.

450g/1lb finely minced
  (ground) lamb
3 large onions, grated
small bunch of flat leaf
  parsley, chopped
5–10ml/1–2 tsp ground cinnamon
5ml/1 tsp ground cumin
pinch of cayenne pepper
40g/1½oz/3 tbsp butter
25g/1oz fresh root ginger, peeled
  and finely chopped
1 hot chilli, seeded and finely
  chopped
pinch of saffron threads
small bunch of fresh coriander
  (cilantro), finely chopped
juice of 1 lemon
300ml/½ pint/1¼ cups water
1 lemon, quartered
salt and ground black pepper

SERVES 4

tagine of lamb
with crunchy country salad

Morocco's hearty tagines are well known for their succulent meat cooked in a combination of honey and warm spices. This delicious recipe is for one of the most traditional and popular tagines, which is best served with a crunchy salad, spiked with chilli to balance the sweetness of the main dish. Offer lots of fresh bread for mopping up the thick, syrupy sauce.

Put the meat in a flameproof casserole or heavy pan. Add the oil, ginger, saffron, cinnamon, onion, garlic and seasoning, then pour in enough water to cover. Heat until just simmering, cover with a lid and simmer gently for about 2 hours, topping up the water if necessary, until the meat is very tender.

Drain the prunes and add them to the tagine. Stir in the honey and simmer for a further 30 minutes, or until the sauce has reduced.

To make the salad, mix the onions, peppers, celery, chillies and garlic in a bowl. Pour the olive oil and lemon juice over the vegetables and toss to coat. Season with salt and add the parsley and mint. Serve the hot lamb tagine with the chilli-laced salad.

1kg/2¼lb boneless shoulder of
    lamb, trimmed and cubed
30–45ml/2–3 tbsp sunflower oil
25g/1oz fresh root ginger, peeled
    and chopped
pinch of saffron threads
10ml/2 tsp ground cinnamon
1 onion, finely chopped
2–3 garlic cloves, chopped
350g/12oz/1½ cups pitted prunes,
    soaked for 1 hour
30ml/2 tbsp clear honey
salt and ground black pepper

FOR THE SALAD
2 onions, chopped
1 red (bell) pepper, seeded
    and chopped
1 green (bell) pepper, seeded
    and chopped
2–3 celery sticks, chopped
2–3 green chillies, seeded
    and chopped
2 garlic cloves, chopped
30ml/2 tbsp olive oil
juice of ½ lemon
small bunch of parsley, chopped
a little mint, chopped

SERVES 6

tagine of beef
with peas and saffron

This tagine is a popular supper dish, and can be made with beef or lamb. Saffron imparts a pungent taste and delicate colour. The peas, tomatoes and tangy lemon added towards the end of cooking enliven the rich, gingery beef mixture and the brown olives finish it off. This is definitely one of the dishes to look out for in Marakesh.

Put the cubed chuck or braising steak in a tagine, flameproof casserole or heavy pan with the olive oil, chopped onion, fresh and ground ginger, cayenne and saffron and season with salt and pepper. Pour in enough water to cover the meat completely and bring to the boil. Then reduce the heat and cover and simmer for about 1½ hours, or until the meat is very tender. Cook for a little longer if necessary.

Add the peas, tomatoes, preserved lemon and olives. Stir well and cook, uncovered, for about 10 minutes, or until the peas are tender and the sauce has reduced. Check the seasoning and serve with bread or plain couscous.

1.2kg/2¼lb chuck steak or
  braising steak, trimmed
  and cubed
30ml/2 tbsp olive oil
1 onion, chopped
25g/1oz fresh root ginger, peeled
  and chopped
5ml/1 tsp ground ginger
pinch of cayenne pepper
pinch of saffron threads
1.2kg/2¼lb shelled fresh peas
2 tomatoes, peeled and chopped
1 preserved lemon, chopped
a handful of brown
  kalamata olives
salt and ground black pepper
bread or couscous, to serve

SERVES 6

roasts, grills & pan-fried dishes

rich and succulent

There is no shortage of fish, meat and poultry in Morocco, where they are grilled or roasted over an open fire, pan-fried or baked in the oven. Roasting, grilling and pan-frying all commence cooking from the outside, leaving the middle of the food moist and tender. Cooking vegetables in this way tends to caramelize their skins and seal in the natural sweetness of their flesh.

Swordfish, tuna, monkfish, sea bream, red mullet, shark, sardines and fresh anchovies are in constant supply, from the Strait of Gibraltar and the Atlantic Ocean. In addition to the ubiquitous beef, lamb and chicken, from the fertile plains and vast tracts of wilderness come pigeon, quail, partridge, hare, rabbit, goat and camel. Fish is commonly marinated in the aromatic spice paste, *chermoula*, and grilled (broiled), pan-fried or baked. Meat and poultry are often grilled or roasted directly over the open fire, particularly in summer.

The most popularly cooked animal in the Muslim world is the sheep. On the day of *Eid el Kebir*, the festival marking the sacrifice of Ismail, sheep are gathered by the roadsides and in the markets for sale as every household will slaughter one and use every bit of it in different dishes. The good cuts of meat are grilled and roasted; the lesser cuts are cooked slowly in tagines

or soups; the head is baked in the local ovens; the trotters are cooked in a tagine with chickpeas; and the bones, joints and gristle are boiled with spices to make the meat conserve, *mrouzia*. Another traditional method for a whole sheep or goat is *mechoui*, cooking on a spit over a charcoal fire burning in a pit. The meat is spiced with garlic and cumin, and cooked very slowly, with frequent basting to ensure it is moist and tender. This is dish and usually reserved for ceremonial occasions.

Whether the main ingredient is fish, meat, poultry or vegetables, you can exploit the ancient methods of roasting, grilling and pan-frying to create dramatic dishes with a modern flavour. Simply swap the traditional pit and open fire for a modern barbecue, oven or heavy pan to create dishes such as chargrilled swordfish steaks with roasted tomatoes, pan-fried quail, or spicy minced (ground) beef kebabs.

summer vegetable kebabs
with harissa and yogurt dip

This simple and tasty vegetarian dish is delicious served with couscous and a fresh, crispy green salad. It also makes an excellent side dish to accompany meat-based main courses. In Morocco today, vegetable and fish kebabs are becoming increasingly popular in fashionable restaurants and households, where there is a tendency to move away from the traditional meat-based meals.

Preheat the grill (broiler) on the hottest setting. Put all the vegetables in a bowl. Mix the olive oil, lemon juice, garlic, ground coriander, cinnamon, honey and salt and pour the mixture over the vegetables. Using your hands, turn the vegetables gently in the marinade, then thread them on to metal skewers. Cook the kebabs under the grill, turning them occasionally until the vegetables are nicely browned all over.

To make the dip, put the yogurt in a bowl and beat in the harissa, making it as fiery as you like by adding more harissa. Add most of the coriander and mint, reserving a little to garnish, and season well with salt and pepper. While they are still hot, slide the vegetables off the skewers and dip them into the yogurt dip before eating. Garnish with the reserved herbs.

Preparing the vegetables
Make sure you cut the aubergines, courgettes and peppers into fairly even-size chunks, so they will all cook at the same rate.

2 aubergines (eggplant), part
  peeled and cut into chunks
2 courgettes (zucchini), cut
  into chunks
2–3 red or green (bell) peppers,
  seeded and cut into chunks
12–16 cherry tomatoes
4 small red onions, quartered
60ml/4 tbsp olive oil
juice of ½ lemon
1 garlic clove, crushed
5ml/1 tsp ground coriander
5ml/1 tsp ground cinnamon
10ml/2 tsp clear honey
5ml/1 tsp salt

FOR THE HARISSA AND
YOGURT DIP
450g/1lb/2 cups Greek
  (US strained plain) yogurt
30–60ml/2–4 tbsp harissa
small bunch of fresh coriander
  (cilantro), finely chopped
small bunch of mint,
  finely chopped
salt and ground black pepper

SERVES 4

butternut squash
with caramelized pink shallots

You can serve this dish as a vegetarian meal on its own, as a side dish or as a topping for couscous. When in season, substitute pumpkin for the squash. A dollop of garlic-flavoured yogurt or a spoonful of harissa goes very well with the squash and shallots. I often serve this dish with a herb-flavoured couscous and a green salad for supper.

Preheat the oven to 200°C/400°F/Gas 6. Place the butternut squash in an ovenproof dish, add the water, cover and bake for about 45 minutes, until tender.

Meanwhile, heat the olive oil and butter in a large heavy pan. Stir in the shallots and cook until they begin to brown. Stir in the garlic and almonds. When the garlic and almonds begin to brown, add the raisins or sultanas. Continue to cook until the shallots and garlic begin to caramelize, then stir in the honey and cinnamon, adding a little water if the mixture becomes too dry. Season well with salt and pepper and remove from the heat.

Cover the squash with the shallot and garlic mixture and return to the oven, uncovered, for a further 15 minutes. Sprinkle with fresh mint and serve with lemon wedges for squeezing over the vegetables.

900g/2lb peeled butternut squash,
    cut into thick slices
120ml/4fl oz/½ cup water
45–60ml/3–4 tbsp olive oil
knob (pat) of butter
16–20 pink shallots, peeled
10–12 garlic cloves, peeled
115g/4oz/1 cup blanched almonds
75g/3oz/generous ½ cup raisins
    or sultanas (golden raisins),
    soaked in warm water for
    15 minutes and drained
30–45ml/2–3 tbsp clear honey
10ml/2 tsp ground cinnamon
small bunch of mint, chopped
salt and ground black pepper
1 lemon, cut into wedges, to serve

SERVES 4

red mullet with chermoula and preserved lemons

The coriander and chilli chermoula marinade gives this dish its distinct flavour. The olives and preserved lemon add a touch of excitement. On their own, these mullet make a delicious appetizer. Served with saffron couscous and a crisp, herb-filled salad, they are delicious as a main course. Choose larger fish if you wish.

30–45ml/2–3 tbsp olive oil, plus
    extra for brushing
1 onion, chopped
1 carrot, chopped
½ preserved lemon, finely
    chopped
4 plum tomatoes, peeled and
    chopped
600ml/1 pint/2½ cups fish stock
    or water
3–4 new potatoes, peeled
    and cubed
4 small red mullet or snapper,
    gutted and filleted
handful of black olives, pitted
    and halved
small bunch of fresh coriander
    (cilantro), chopped
small bunch of mint, chopped
salt and ground black pepper

FOR THE CHERMOULA
small bunch of fresh coriander
    (cilantro), finely chopped
2–3 garlic cloves, chopped
5–10ml/1–2 tsp ground cumin
pinch of saffron threads
60ml/4 tbsp olive oil
juice of 1 lemon
1 hot red chilli, seeded
    and chopped
5ml/1 tsp salt

SERVES 4

To make the chermoula, pound the ingredients in a mortar with a pestle, or process them together in a food processor, then set aside.

Heat the olive oil in a pan. Add the onion and carrot and cook until softened but not browned. Stir in half the preserved lemon, along with 30ml/2 tbsp of the chermoula, the tomatoes and the stock or water. Bring to the boil, then reduce the heat, cover and simmer for about 30 minutes. Add the potatoes and simmer for a further 10 minutes, until they are tender.

Preheat the grill (broiler) on the hottest setting and brush a baking sheet or grill pan with oil. Brush the fish fillets with olive oil and a little of the chermoula. Season with salt and pepper, then place the fillets, skin-side up, on the sheet or pan and cook under the grill for 5–6 minutes.

Meanwhile, stir the olives, the remaining chermoula and preserved lemon into the sauce and check the seasoning. Serve the fish fillets in wide bowls, spoon the sauce over and sprinkle liberally with chopped coriander and mint.

grilled fish in vine leaves with sweet and sour chilli dipping sauce

Almost any kind of firm, white fish will do for these kebabs. The fish is first marinated in chermoula and then wrapped in vine leaves to seal in the flavours. The vine-leaf parcel becomes crisp when cooked to contrast with its succulent, aromatic contents. The piquant, sweet and sour dipping sauce complements these crisp parcels perfectly.

about 30 preserved vine leaves
4–5 large white fish fillets,
　skinned, such as haddock, ling
　or monkfish

FOR THE CHERMOULA
small bunch of fresh coriander
　(cilantro), finely chopped
2–3 garlic cloves, chopped
5–10ml/1–2 tsp ground cumin
60ml/4 tbsp olive oil
juice of 1 lemon
salt

FOR THE DIPPING SAUCE
50ml/2fl oz/¼ cup white wine
　vinegar or lemon juice
115g/4oz/½ cup caster
　(superfine) sugar
15–30ml/1–2 tbsp water
pinch of saffron threads
1 onion, finely chopped
2 garlic cloves, finely chopped
2–3 spring onions (scallions),
　finely sliced
25g/1oz fresh root ginger, peeled
　and grated
2 hot red or green chillies, seeded
　and finely sliced
small bunch fresh coriander
　(cilantro), finely chopped
small bunch of mint, finely
　chopped

SERVES 4

To make the chermoula, pound the ingredients in a mortar with a pestle, or process them together in a food processor, then set aside.

Rinse the vine leaves in a bowl, then soak them in cold water. Remove any bones from the fish and cut each fillet into about eight bitesize pieces. Coat the pieces of fish in the chermoula, cover and chill for 1 hour.

Meanwhile, prepare the dipping sauce. Heat the vinegar or lemon juice with the sugar and water until the sugar has dissolved. Bring to the boil and boil for about 1 minute, then leave to cool. Add the remaining ingredients and mix well to combine. Spoon the sauce into small individual bowls and set aside.

Drain the vine leaves and pat dry on kitchen paper. Lay a vine leaf flat on the work surface and place a piece of marinated fish in the centre. Fold the edges of the leaf over the fish, then wrap up the fish and leaf into a small parcel. Repeat with the remaining pieces of fish and vine leaves. Thread the parcels on to kebab skewers and brush with any leftover marinade.

Heat the grill (broiler) on the hottest setting and cook the kebabs for 2–3 minutes on each side. Serve immediately, with the sweet and sour chilli sauce for dipping.

spiced sardines with grapefruit and fennel salad

Sardines spiced with cumin and coriander are popular in the coastal regions of Morocco, both in restaurants and as street food. In Tangier, I ate them from a street stall, where they were cleaned and smeared with a spicy paste, dredged with flour and deep-fried, then sandwiched between two bits of bread with a handful of fresh coriander.

Rinse the sardines and pat them dry on kitchen paper, then rub inside and out with a little coarse salt. In a bowl, mix the grated onion with the olive oil, cinnamon, ground roasted cumin and coriander, paprika and black pepper. Make several slashes into the flesh of the sardines and smear the onion and spice mixture all over the fish, inside and out and into the gashes. Leave the sardines to stand for about 1 hour to allow the flavours of the spices to penetrate the flesh.

Meanwhile, prepare the salad. Peel the grapefruits with a knife, removing all the pith and peel in neat strips down the outside of the fruit. Cut between the membranes to remove the segments of fruit intact. Cut each grapefruit segment in half, place in a bowl and sprinkle with salt. Trim the fennel, cut it in half lengthways and slice finely. Add the fennel to the grapefruit with the spring onions, cumin and olive oil. Toss lightly, then garnish with the olives.

Preheat the grill (broiler) or barbecue. Cook the sardines for 3–4 minutes on each side, basting with any leftover marinade. Sprinkle with fresh coriander and serve immediately, with lemon wedges for squeezing over and the refreshing, grapefruit and fennel salad.

12 fresh sardines, gutted
1 onion, grated
60–90ml/4–6 tbsp olive oil
5ml/1 tsp ground cinnamon
10ml/2 tsp cumin seeds, roasted
  and ground
10ml/2 tsp coriander seeds,
  roasted and ground
5ml/1 tsp paprika
5ml/1 tsp ground black pepper
small bunch of fresh coriander
  (cilantro), chopped
coarse salt
2 lemons, cut into wedges,
  to serve

FOR THE SALAD
2 ruby grapefruits
5ml/1 tsp sea salt
1 fennel bulb
2–3 spring onions (scallions),
  finely sliced
2.5ml/½ tsp ground roasted
  cumin
30–45ml/2–3 tbsp olive oil
handful of black olives

SERVES 4–6

griddled swordfish with roasted tomatoes and cinnamon

The sun-ripened tomatoes of Morocco are naturally full of flavour and sweetness, and when roasted with sugar and spices they simply melt in the mouth. As an accompaniment to chargrilled fish or poultry, they are sensational. These delectable tomatoes can also be stored in sealed containers in the refrigerator, ideal for impromptu barbecues.

Preheat the oven to 110°C/225°F/Gas ¼. Place the tomatoes on a baking sheet. Sprinkle with the cinnamon, saffron and orange flower water. Trickle half the oil over, being sure to moisten every tomato half, and sprinkle with sugar. Place the tray in the bottom of the oven and cook the tomatoes for about 3 hours, then turn the oven off and leave them to cool.

Brush the remaining olive oil over the swordfish steaks and season with salt and pepper. Lightly oil a pre-heated cast-iron griddle and cook the steaks for 3–4 minutes on each side. Sprinkle the chopped preserved lemon and coriander over the steaks towards the end of the cooking time.

In a separate pan, fry the almonds in the butter until golden and sprinkle them over the tomatoes. Then serve the steaks immediately with the tomatoes.

Variations

If swordfish steaks are not available, tuna or shark steaks can be cooked in the same way with excellent results. Or, if you prefer, try the recipe with a lean sirloin or thinly cut fillet steak (beef tenderloin). The flavours lift the meat beautifully.

1kg/2¼lb large vine or plum
  tomatoes, peeled, halved
  and seeded
5–10ml/1–2 tsp ground cinnamon
pinch of saffron threads
15ml/1 tbsp orange flower water
60ml/4 tbsp olive oil
45–60ml/3–4 tbsp sugar
4 × 225g/8oz swordfish steaks
rind of ½ preserved lemon,
  finely chopped
small bunch of fresh coriander
  (cilantro), finely chopped
handful of blanched almonds
knob (pat) of butter
salt and ground black pepper

SERVES 4

seared tuna with ginger, chilli and watercress salad

Tuna steaks are wonderful seared and served slightly rare with a punchy sauce or salad. In this recipe the salad is served just warm as a bed for the tender tuna. Add a dab of harissa as a condiment to create a dish that will transport you to the warmth of the North African coastline. If you can't get tuna, try using salmon steaks instead.

30ml/2 tbsp olive oil
5ml/1 tsp harissa
5ml/1 tsp clear honey
4 × 200g/7oz tuna steaks
salt and ground black pepper
lemon wedges, to serve

FOR THE SALAD
30ml/2 tbsp olive oil
a little butter
25g/1oz fresh root ginger, peeled
    and finely sliced
2 garlic cloves, finely sliced
2 green chillies, seeded and
    finely sliced
6 spring onions (scallions), cut into
    bitesize pieces
2 large handfuls of watercress
juice of ½ lemon

SERVES 4

Mix the olive oil, harissa, honey and salt, and rub it over the tuna steaks. Heat a frying pan, grease it with a little oil and sear the tuna steaks for about 2 minutes on each side. They should still be pink on the inside.

Keep the tuna warm while you quickly prepare the salad: heat the olive oil and butter in a heavy pan. Add the ginger, garlic, chillies and spring onions, cook until the mixture begins to colour, then add the watercress. When the watercress begins to wilt, toss in the lemon juice and season well with salt and plenty of ground black pepper.

Tip the warm salad on to a serving dish or individual plates. Slice the tuna steaks and arrange on top of the salad. Serve immediately with lemon wedges for squeezing over.

Seared shellfish
Prawns (shrimp) and scallops can be cooked in the same way. The shellfish will just need to be cooked through briefly – too long and they will become rubbery.

salads &
side dishes

broad bean salad and carrot salad

Throughout the Middle East, North Africa and the Mediterranean region, broad beans are a popular addition to salads and rice dishes but, in Morocco, the addition of preserved lemons gives this salad a distinct and appealing taste. The refreshing carrot salad is often served as an appetizer but, if you prefer, serve it warm for supper with tangy, garlic-flavoured yogurt.

To make the broad bean salad, bring a large pan of salted water to the boil. Meanwhile, pod the beans. Put the beans in the pan and boil for about 2 minutes, then drain and refresh the beans under cold running water. Drain well. Slip off and discard the thick outer skin to reveal the smooth, bright green beans underneath.

Put the beans in a heavy pan and add the olive oil, lemon juice, garlic, cumin and paprika. Cook the beans gently over a low heat for about 10 minutes, then season to taste with salt and pepper and leave to cool in the pan.

Tip the beans into a serving bowl, scraping all the juices from the pan. Toss in the fresh coriander and preserved lemon and garnish with the black olives.

To make the carrot salad, steam the carrots over boiling water for about 15 minutes, or until tender. While they are still warm, toss the carrots in a serving bowl with the olive oil, lemon juice, garlic and sugar. Season to taste, then add the cumin seeds, cinnamon and paprika. Finally, toss in the fresh coriander and mint, and serve warm or at room temperature.

Roasting cumin seeds
Stir the cumin seeds in a heavy pan over a low heat until they change colour slightly and emit a warm, nutty aroma. Be careful not to burn them.

FOR THE BROAD BEAN SALAD
2kg/4½lb broad (fava) beans in the pod
60–75ml/4–5 tbsp olive oil
juice of ½ lemon
2 garlic cloves, chopped
5ml/1 tsp ground cumin
10ml/2 tsp paprika
small bunch of fresh coriander (cilantro), finely chopped
1 preserved lemon, chopped
handful of black olives, to garnish
salt and ground black pepper

SERVES 4

FOR THE CARROT SALAD
450g/1lb carrots, cut into sticks
30–45ml/2–3 tbsp olive oil
juice of 1 lemon
2–3 garlic cloves, crushed
10ml/2 tsp sugar
5–10ml/1–2 tsp cumin seeds, roasted
5ml/1 tsp ground cinnamon
5ml/1 tsp paprika
small bunch of fresh coriander (cilantro), finely chopped
small bunch of mint, finely chopped
salt and ground black pepper

SERVES 4

sweets,
pastries
& drinks

sweet treats

The most common way to end the daily meal in the home is with a simple platter of fresh fruit. However, there is also a wonderful range of simple desserts, often based on fruit or milk, as well as wonderful sweet pastries and cakes that are enjoyed at other times of the day.

To dine Moroccan style, after wiping away the last grains of couscous from the fingers, select from the season's fruit. The choice of fresh fruits is vast, ranging from different types of dates, grapes and sweet melons, to strawberries, peaches, apricots, ruby-red pomegranates, yellow plums, plump cherries, bursting figs, white and purple mulberries, pineapples, mangoes, prickly pears and cactus fruit. Some fruits, such as quinces and plums, lend themselves to poaching in syrup with spices, producing delicate tastes and ancient methods of preserving.

More homely desserts and sweet snacks are often based on creamy yogurt or milk. The yogurt is sprinkled with sugar or drenched in honey and, in modern households, it is often served with fruit. The milk puddings are also quite plain, often lifted with a touch of saffron or flower water.

Sweet pastries and cakes are more often enjoyed as snacks from a street stall or pastry shop. Some are complicated and time-consuming to make, requiring special kneading and techniques that require years of practise. Today's busy cooks buy ready-prepared ouarka, the paper-thin dough used to make many of the sweet pastries. If there is a good pastry shop in the neighbourhood, it is even easier to pop out and buy a ready-made cake or sweet pastry dish.

There are rich pastries for feast days; sticky, honey cakes and fried pastries bathed in scented syrup for Ramadan; simple cookies decorated with nuts to offer to guests as a mark of hospitality; and cakes and pastries filled with almond paste for a touch of refinement. One of the most famous Moroccan pastries is M'hanncha, coiled like a snake and sprinkled with cinnamon and icing (confectioners') sugar.

watermelon and spiced orange granitas

These refreshing granitas are glorious in the summer, and particularly welcome as a dessert to follow a spicy tagine. Fruits such as the pineapple, mango and banana, used here, can be cooked under a grill or on a griddle. Make the granitas the day before they are required. If you close your eyes while eating, the flavours will transport you to a beach under the hot Moroccan sun.

To make the watermelon granita, purée the watermelon flesh in a blender. Put the sugar and water in a pan and stir until dissolved. Bring to the boil, simmer for 5 minutes, then cool.

Stir in the lemon juice, orange flower water and cinnamon, then beat in the watermelon purée. Pour the mixture into a bowl; place in the freezer. Stir every 15 minutes for 2 hours and then at intervals for 1 hour, so that the mixture freezes but is slushy.

To make the spiced orange granita, heat the water and sugar together in a pan with the cloves, stirring until the sugar has dissolved, then bring to the boil and boil for about 5 minutes. Leave to cool and stir in the ginger, cinnamon, orange juice and orange flower water.

Remove the cloves, then pour the mixture into a bowl, cover and place in the freezer. Freeze as for the watermelon granita.

To serve, peel, core and slice the pineapple. Peel the mango, cut the flesh off the stone (pit) in thick slices. Peel and halve the bananas. Preheat the grill (broiler) on the hottest setting. Arrange the fruit on a baking sheet. Sprinkle with icing sugar and grill for 3–4 minutes until slightly softened and lightly browned. Arrange the fruit on a serving platter and scoop the granitas into dishes. Serve immediately.

1 pineapple
1 mango
2 bananas
45–60ml/3–4 tbsp icing (confectioners') sugar

FOR THE WATERMELON GRANITA
1kg/2¼lb watermelon, seeds removed
250g/9oz/1¼ cups caster (superfine) sugar
150ml/¼ pint/⅔ cup water
juice of ½ lemon
15ml/1 tbsp orange flower water
2.5ml/½ tsp ground cinnamon

FOR THE SPICED ORANGE GRANITA
900ml/1½ pints/3¾ cups water
350g/12oz/1¾ cups sugar
5–6 cloves
5ml/1 tsp ground ginger
2.5ml/½ tsp ground cinnamon
600ml/1 pint/2½ cups fresh orange juice
15ml/1 tbsp orange flower water

SERVES 6–8

almond and pistachio ice creams

Creamy green pistachio ice cream and snowy almond ice cream are legendary ancient culinary delights of the Arab Empire, adopted from the Persians. These refreshing modern versions are equally cooling in the heat of the day and provide a memorable finale for a Moroccan meal. All ice creams can be made and whisked by hand but, for a really smooth texture, you need to rely on the modern ice cream machine.

FOR THE ALMOND ICE CREAM
150g/5oz/1¼ cups blanched almonds, finely ground
300ml/½ pint/1¼ cups milk
300ml/½ pint/1¼ cups double (heavy) cream
4 egg yolks
175g/6oz/generous ¾ cup caster (superfine) sugar
30–45ml/2–3 tbsp orange flower water
2–3 drops almond essence (extract)

FOR THE PISTACHIO ICE CREAM
150g/5oz/1¼ cups pistachio nuts, blanched and finely ground
300ml/½ pint/1¼ cups milk
300ml/½ pint/1¼ cups double (heavy) cream
4 egg yolks
175g/6oz/generous ¾ cup sugar
30–45ml/2–3 tbsp rose water
green food colouring (optional)

SERVES 6–8

To make the almond ice cream, put the almonds in a pan with the milk and cream, and bring to the boil. In a large bowl, beat the egg yolks with the sugar, then pour in the hot milk and cream, beating all the time. Pour the mixture back into the pan and stir over a low heat until it thickens slightly. Take care not to overheat the custard as, if it approaches simmering point, it will curdle.

Stir in the orange flower water and almond essence, and leave the mixture to cool. Pour the cold mixture into a bowl or freezer container and chill, then freeze. Whisk the mixture thoroughly after about 1 hour, when it should be icy around the edges. Continue to freeze the ice cream, whisking two or three times, until it is smooth and very thick. Then return it to the freezer and leave for several hours or overnight. Alternatively, churn the mixture in an ice cream maker.

Make the pistachio ice cream in the same way as the almond ice cream, using the pistachio nuts instead of the almonds and rose water instead of the orange flower water and almond essence. Add a little green food colouring to the pistachio ice cream, if you like.

Remove both batches of ice cream from the freezer 10–15 minutes before serving and allow to soften slightly.

poached pears in scented honey syrup

Fruit has been poached in honey since ancient times. The Romans did it, as did the Persians, Arabs, Moors and Ottomans. The Moroccans continue the tradition today, adding a little orange rind or aniseed, or even lavender to give a subtle flavouring. Delicate and pretty to look at, these scented pears provide an exquisite finishing touch to a Moroccan meal.

Heat the honey and lemon juice in a heavy pan that will hold the pears snugly. Stir over a gentle heat until the honey has dissolved. Add the water, saffron threads, cinnamon stick and flowers from 1–2 lavender heads. Bring the mixture to the boil, then reduce the heat and simmer for 5 minutes.

Peel the pears, leaving the stalks attached. Add the pears to the pan and simmer for 20 minutes, turning and basting at regular intervals, until they are tender. Leave the pears to cool in the syrup and serve at room temperature, decorated with a few lavender flowers.

45ml/3 tbsp clear honey
juice of 1 lemon
250ml/8fl oz/1 cup water
pinch of saffron threads
1 cinnamon stick
2–3 dried lavender heads
4 firm pears

SERVES 4

apricot parcels with honey glaze

These parcels can be made with dried apricots poached in syrup and then stuffed, but I prefer to use fresh fruit as it lends a juicy tartness to the otherwise sweet dish, which the dried fruit does not possess. Roll or twist the filo parcels into any shape or size, just make sure you leave them open, so that the fruit and pastry benefit from the honey glaze.

Preheat the oven to 180°C/350°F/Gas 4. Using your hands, a blender or food processor, bind the almonds, sugar and orange flower water or rose water to a soft paste.

Take small walnut-size lumps of the paste and roll them into balls. Press a ball of paste into each slit apricot and gently squeeze the fruit closed. Place a stuffed apricot on a piece of filo pastry, fold up the sides to secure the fruit and twist the ends to form an open boat. Repeat with the remaining apricots and filo pastry.

Place the filo parcels in a shallow ovenproof dish and drizzle the honey over them. Bake for 20–25 minutes, until the pastry is crisp and the fruit has browned on top. Serve hot or cold with cream, crème fraîche, or a spoonful of yogurt.

200g/7oz/1¾ cups blanched
   almonds, ground
115g/4oz/⅔ cup sugar
30–45ml/2–3 tbsp orange flower
   or rose water
12 apricots, slit and stoned (pitted)
3–4 sheets filo pastry, cut into
   12 circles or squares
30ml/2 tbsp clear honey

SERVES 6

sweet couscous with rose-scented fruit compote

Aside from its savoury role, couscous is also eaten as a dessert or a nourishing breakfast. This sweet, filling and nutritious dish is lovely served with a dried fruit compote and it is particularly popular with children in the mountainous regions of Morocco where the winters can be long and cold. Make it as sweet and creamy as you like. It makes a delicious snack when the weather is chilly.

Prepare the fruit compote a couple of days in advance. Put the dried fruit and almonds in a bowl and pour in just enough water to cover. Gently stir in the sugar and rose water, and add the cinnamon stick. Cover and leave the fruit and nuts to soak for 48 hours, during which time the water and sugar will form a lovely golden-coloured syrup.

To make the couscous, bring the water to the boil in a pan. Stir in the couscous and raisins, and cook gently for 1–2 minutes, until the water has been absorbed. Remove the pan from the heat, cover tightly and leave the couscous to steam for 10–15 minutes. Meanwhile, poach the compote over a gentle heat until warmed through.

Tip the couscous into a bowl and separate the grains with your fingertips. Melt the butter and pour it over the couscous. Sprinkle the sugar over the top then, using your fingertips, rub the butter and sugar into the couscous. Divide the mixture among six bowls.

Heat the milk and cream together in a small, heavy pan until just about to boil, then pour the mixture over the couscous. Serve immediately, with the dried fruit compote.

Variations
The couscous can be served on its own, drizzled with clear or melted honey instead of with the dried fruit compote. The compote is also delicious served chilled on its own or with yogurt.

300ml/½ pint/1¼ cups water
225g/8oz/1⅓ cups medium
    couscous
50g/2oz/scant ⅓ cup raisins
50g/2oz/¼ cup butter
50g/2oz/¼ cup sugar
120ml/4fl oz/½ cup milk
120ml/4fl oz/½ cup double
    (heavy) cream

FOR THE FRUIT COMPOTE
225g/8oz/2 cups dried apricots
225g/8oz/1 cup pitted prunes
115/4oz/¾ cup sultanas
    (golden raisins)
115g/4oz/1 cup blanched almonds
175g/6oz/generous ¾ cup sugar
30ml/2 tbsp rose water
1 cinnamon stick

SERVES 6

yogurt cake with pistachio nuts, crème fraîche and passion fruit

Some yogurt cakes are dry and served with tea, others are bathed in lemon syrup and served at room temperature, and then there is this type, which is delicious warm or chilled with a dollop of crème fraîche or yogurt and a spoonful of fresh passion fruit. In Morocco this type of moist cake isn't necessarily reserved for dessert; it can be enjoyed at any time of day.

Preheat the oven to 180°C/350°F/Gas 4. Line a 25cm/10in square, heatproof dish with greaseproof (waxed) paper and grease well.

Beat the egg yolks with two-thirds of the sugar, until pale and fluffy. Beat in the vanilla seeds and stir in the yogurt, lemon rind and juice, and the flour. In a separate bowl, whisk the egg whites until stiff, then gradually whisk in the rest of the sugar to form soft peaks. Fold the whisked whites into the yogurt mixture. Turn the mixture into the lined dish.

Place the dish in a roasting pan and pour in cold water to come about halfway up the outside of the dish. Bake for about 20 minutes until the mixture is risen and just set. Sprinkle the pistachio nuts over the cake and cook for a further 20 minutes, until browned on top.

Serve the cake warm or chilled with crème fraîche and a spoonful of passion fruit drizzled over the top. Alternatively, sprinkle with a few summer berries such as redcurrants, blackcurrants and blueberries.

3 eggs, separated
75g/3oz/scant ½ cup caster
  (superfine) sugar
seeds from 2 vanilla pods (beans)
300ml/½ pint/1¼ cups Greek
  (US strained plain) yogurt
grated rind and juice of 1 lemon
scant 15ml/1 tbsp plain
  (all-purpose) flour
handful of pistachio nuts,
  roughly chopped
60–90ml/4–6 tbsp crème fraîche
  and 4–6 fresh passion fruit or
  50g/2oz/½ cup summer berries,
  to serve

SERVES 4–6

m'hanncha

The snake, or *m'hanncha* as it is known in Arabic, is the most famous, traditional sweet dish in Morocco. This coiled pastry looks impressive and tastes divine. The crisp, buttery filo is filled with almond paste that has been scented with cinnamon and orange flower water. Serve *m'hanncha* as a dessert or as an afternoon snack with mint tea. Every Moroccan, whether young or old, has grown up with this pastry, so a book on Moroccan food would not be complete without it.

115g/4oz/1 cup blanched almonds
300g/11oz/2¾ cups ground
  almonds
50g/2oz/½ cup icing
  (confectioners') sugar
115g/4oz/⅔ cup caster
  (superfine) sugar
115g/4oz/½ cup butter, softened,
  plus 20g/¾oz for cooking nuts
5–10ml/1–2 tsp ground cinnamon
15ml/1 tbsp orange flower water
3–4 sheets filo pastry
1 egg yolk

FOR THE TOPPING
icing (confectioners') sugar
ground cinnamon

SERVES 8–10

Fry the blanched almonds in a little butter until golden brown, then pound them using a pestle and mortar until they resemble coarse breadcrumbs. Place the nuts in a bowl and add the ground almonds, icing sugar, caster sugar, butter, cinnamon and orange flower water. Use your hands to form the mixture into a smooth paste. Cover and chill in the refrigerator for about 30 minutes.

Preheat the oven to 180°C/350°F/Gas 4. Open out the sheets of filo pastry, keeping them in a pile so they do not dry out, and brush the top one with a little melted butter. Take lumps of the almond paste and roll them into fingers. Place them end to end along the long edge of the top sheet of filo, then roll the filo up into a roll the thickness of your thumb, tucking in the ends to stop the filling oozing out. Repeat with the other sheets of filo, until all the filling is used up.

Grease a large round baking pan or the widest baking sheet you can find. Lift one of the filo rolls in both hands and gently push it together from both ends, like an accordion, to relax the pastry before coiling it in the centre of the pan or baking sheet. Do the same with the other rolls, placing them end to end to form a tight coil like a snake.

Mix the egg yolk with a little water and brush this over the pastry, then bake for 30–35 minutes, until crisp and lightly browned. Top the freshly cooked pastry with a liberal sprinkling of icing sugar, and add lines of cinnamon like the spokes of a wheel. Serve at room temperature.

basic flavourings & ingredients

essential flavours

At the heart of modern Moroccan cooking are the spice mixes and flavourings that have been used for centuries. It is worth preparing some of the following basic recipes, as traditional ingredients such as preserved lemons, hot *harissa* paste and *chermoula* marinade are essential if you wish to create authentic Moroccan dishes. Most of these classic flavourings can now be purchased ready-made but they are simple to make at home.

Preserved lemons are one of the most important ingredients used in Moroccan cuisine. With their tender rinds, jam-like consistency and intense flavour, they impart a distinctive taste to many dishes. The lemons can be preserved in salt, brine or oil, or they can be pickled, but salt and lemon juice is the most popular method and give a wonderful result.

Traditional spice mixes such as the complex, heaven-scented *ras el hanout* also play an important role in many recipes. Many of the spices so intricately entwined in the cuisine of Morocco came to the region with the Arabs. These skilled seafarers and traders brought pungent spices from China, the

East Indies, Persia, Egypt and Zanzibar. Cinnamon, ginger, cumin and coriander are perhaps the most traditional spices in Moroccan cooking, along with chillies and paprika from the New World. Just across the water in Spain, these same flavours feature in the cooking of Andalucia. Two spice mixes that play a key role in Moroccan food but originate from elsewhere are *tabil* from Tunisia and *zahtar* from the Middle East.

Other important ingredients that lend their distinctive, and typically Moroccan, character to dishes are the unusual-tasting aged butter *smen* and the paper-thin sheets of *ouarka* that are used to make traditional pies and pastries.

grapefruit and fennel, 94–5
lentil with red onion and garlic, 113
pale courgette and cauliflower, 14–5
sautéed herb salad with chilli and preserved lemon, 117
sardines with grapefruit and fennel salad, 94–5
semolina: beghrir, 38–9
sesame-coated majoun, 46
shallots: butternut squash with caramelized pink shallots, 88–9
smen, 157
soups, 28–33
spinach: sautéed with apple, pine nuts and cream, 120–1

savoury cigars and triangles, 44–5
spring rolls with chicken, spring onions and almonds, 54–5
squid: pan-fried baby squid with, 22
summer vegetable kebabs, 86–7
sweet and sour chilli dipping sauce, 92–3
swordfish with roasted tomatoes and cinnamon, 96–7

T
tabil, 157
tagines, 59–61, 68–81
tomatoes: bus-station kefta, 56–7
chunky tomato soup, 32–3

swordfish with roasted tomatoes and cinnamon, 96–7
tagine of butter beans, cherry tomatoes and olives, 124–5
tagine of monkfish, potatoes, cherry tomatoes and olives, 70–1
tuna: seared tuna with ginger, chilli and watercress salad, 98–9

V
vegetables, 111
Casablancan couscous with roasted summer vegetables, 62–3
summer vegetable kebabs, 86–7
vine leaves, grilled fish in, 92–3

W
walnuts: sesame-coated majoun, 46
watercress: seared tuna with ginger, chilli and watercress salad, 98–9
watermelon granita, 130–1

Y
yam, tagine of carrots, prunes and, 122–3
yogurt: harissa and yogurt dip, 86–7
minted pomegranate yogurt, 134–5
yogurt cake, 144–5

Z
zahtar, 16, 157

This edition is published by Aquamarine, an imprint of Anness Publishing Ltd Hermes House, 88–89 Blackfriars Road, London SE1 8HA; tel. 020 7401 2077 fax 020 7633 9499; www.aquamarinebooks.com; www.annesspublishing.com

If you like the images in this book and would like to investigate using them for publishing, promotions or advertising, please visit our website www.practicalpictures.com for more information.

UK agent: The Manning Partnership Ltd;
tel. 01225 478444; fax 01225 478440; sales@manning-partnership.co.uk
UK distributor: Grantham Book Services Ltd;
tel. 01476 541080; fax 01476 541061; orders@gbs.tbs-ltd.co.uk
North American agent/distributor: National Book Network;
tel. 301 459 3366; fax 301 429 5746; www.nbnbooks.com
Australian agent/distributor: Pan Macmillan Australia;
tel. 1300 135 113; fax 1300 135 103; customer.service@macmillan.com.au
New Zealand agent/distributor: David Bateman Ltd;
tel. (09) 415 7664; fax (09) 415 8892

Publisher: Joanna Lorenz
Managing Editor: Linda Fraser
Senior Editor: Susannah Blake
Design: SteersMcGillan Ltd
Photographer: Martin Brigdale
Stylist: Helen Trent
Home Economists: Lucy McKelvie and Linda Tubby
Production Controller: Ann Childers

ETHICAL TRADING POLICY

Notes

Bracketed terms are intended for American readers.
For all recipes, quantities are given in both metric and imperial measures and, where appropriate, in standard cups and spoons. Follow one set of measures, but not a mixture, because they are not interchangeable.
Australian standard tablespoons are 20ml. Australian readers should use 3 tsp in place of 1 tbsp for measuring small quantities.
American pints are 16fl oz/2 cups. American readers should use 20fl oz/ 2.5 cups in place of 1 pint when measuring liquids.
Electric oven temperatures in this book are for conventional ovens. When using a fan oven, the temperature will probably need to be reduced by about 10–20°C/20–40°F. Since ovens vary, you should check with your manufacturer's instruction book for guidance.
Medium (US large) eggs are used unless otherwise stated.
Standard spoon and cup measures are level. 1 tsp = 5ml, 1 tbsp = 15ml, 1 cup = 250ml/8fl oz.

Author's Acknowledgements
I always enjoy my culinary journeys in North Africa and the Middle East and have received help and hospitality from more people than I could possibly thank here. For research, *Traditional Moroccan Cooking* by Zette Guinaudeau was a delight.

For the best spices and spice mixes from around the world, please contact: Seasoned Pioneers Ltd
101 Summers Road
Brunswick Business Park
Liverpool L3 4BJ
Tel/Fax: 44 (0) 151 709 9330
Freephone: 0800 0682348

Main front cover image shows Tagine of Yam, Carrots and Prunes – for recipe, see page 123